The Heart of Community

Amy Eldridge

Copyright 2021 by Amy Eldridge

All rights reserved.

Printed in the United States of America

No part of this book may be used or reproduced in any manner without permission except in the case of brief quotations embodied in critical articles and reviews.

First edition

Cover photograph by In Sokleng

Edited by Sheri Russon and Marcy Selander

The names of the children in this book have been changed to protect their privacy.

ISBN 9798519566483

To the entire LWB community -

My deepest gratitude for all the good you make possible

Marla —

So grateful to you for being part of the LWB family!

Amy

The Heart of Community

Introduction

With each passing year, I grow in the wisdom of just how little I truly know about the world. Even sitting down to write the next book of the LWB story makes me feel a bit uneasy. So often people who write on a certain topic are considered "experts," and that's definitely not a descriptor to be applied to me, even after working in the international charity field for almost two decades.

One thing I have learned in this life so far, however, is that the best way to create any authentic change is to first listen, ponder, and then listen some more. I worry sometimes that social media is making the gift of truly hearing each other much harder for us all, as people are increasingly asked to pick definitive sides, and our engagement with one another is often reduced to clicking "like" or swiping left. The pandemic has only added to the loss of our personal interaction, at a time when I feel what all of us really want in our lives is genuine connection.

When I first wrote *The Heart of an Orphan*, I hoped that the children's stories I told would help share the message that, regardless of a child's location or needs, they are infinitely worthy of being loved. Indeed, it's the motto of Love Without Boundaries, the charity I helped found in 2003 that "Every Child Counts." As we've grown and expanded our work to additional countries around the world, another key belief we embrace is the vital importance of community. From the very beginning of LWB, we've worked in partnership with local citizens on the ground to change the lives of vulnerable children. In fact, every LWB project is run by people who grew up in the region where we are working, as the best solutions to the challenges that children face are developed locally. We listen closely before beginning our work together, empowering each other to create lasting impact.

What qualifies as a healthy community, though? Community is used to describe our neighborhoods and geographic locations, as well as online forums for different interests. What makes a community strong? What elements help bring a real sense of belonging to something bigger than oneself? Through the stories in the chapters to come, I'd like to share what community has meant for LWB.

Chapter 1: Sacrifice

There is no higher calling than to give love to people. Giving connects us to others, creating stronger communities and helping to build a happier society for everyone. It's why I decided to sacrifice all my heart to helping others and sold myself to this nation.

In Sokleng, LWB-Cambodia Director

If you read the first book in the LWB story, *The Heart of an Orphan*, you know it all started with an orphaned baby in China who needed heart surgery. The effort to save his life launched a movement to bring hope and healing to vulnerable children throughout the country. For the first 13 years, all our programs were focused solely on kids in China. In 2016, our board of directors made the decision to live out our name and expand our critical work in medical support, foster care, nutrition, and education to help children in other countries.

As discussions continued, another location in Asia seemed like a natural progression. Despite countless different cultures, we'd at least have projects on the same continent, right? Exactly where to expand became the biggest question. I spent the next several months carefully researching the work that small local NGOs in Asia were doing to help orphaned children. I had narrowed our search down to three domestic charities in Thailand when I came across the book *Preventing Human Trafficking* by Dr. Robert Spires. He had worked with several children's NGOs in Thailand, whose names I recognized from my research. I quickly sent off an introductory message to him and was surprised when he replied a few minutes later asking if I wanted to jump on a call.

He could not have been more kind, giving me greater insight into some of the challenges facing impoverished children in Southeast Asia. At the end of our call, he paused for a moment before finally saying, "I don't want to be presumptuous, but I'd love to tell you about a young man just across the Thai border in Cambodia. I met him on my travels, and he's doing some pretty amazing work with vulnerable kids, with next to no resources."

I listened carefully, and at the end of our call I was fully convinced that I needed to meet this remarkable young man, Mr. In Sokleng, in person. I smile now when I think of how quickly the plans were made. Just three weeks after the call with Dr. Spires, I landed in Bangkok and began the journey to the notorious border town of Poipet, Cambodia. Back when I traveled in 2016, Poipet was described online as a crime-filled gambling mecca, with nicknames like "sin city" and "the wild, wild west." The Poipet TripAdvisor pages actually had a warning label which read, "Scam central. An unholy welcome to an otherwise fascinating country."

At the time, the only way to cross the border from Thailand to Cambodia was on foot. Every online article I found was filled with comments from tourists describing Dante levels of harassment and scams they encountered while trying to exit the Thai checkpoint and enter Cambodia. Even after reading several "definitive guides" on how to navigate the border successfully, I was still pretty frazzled by the time the final clearance stamp was entered in my passport. My friends and I exited Poipet's checkpoint building onto the main road and were met by a sea of swerving motorcycles, street vendors pushing wooden carts, and people of all ages begging. We stood trying to process our first moments in Cambodia while wondering how we would ever find the person we were supposed to meet. Just then, I looked across the street and saw a young man with an enormous smile waving happily at us. I knew in an instant it had to be Leng. His whole face radiated kindness.

The two of us had already spoken online with each other several times, but it was wonderful to finally be able to sit down together in person to hear more of his story. While he is soft spoken and even shy when talking, you only need to spend a few moments with Leng to sense his determined passion to help children living in the rural villages outside his city.

Like so many in Cambodia, Leng's family had been deeply impacted by the war with the Khmer Rouge, a brutal period in the 1970s which resulted in the deaths of almost two million people, or one quarter of the country's population. Cambodia became, in far too simple terms, a country of trauma. The effects of the civil war still impact Cambodian society today. Life in the impoverished rural villages remains difficult, with many people having no electricity or clean water, and a staggering 40% of children under the age of five being malnourished.

It embarrasses me to admit how extraordinarily little I knew about this catastrophic period of history. I had not been taught about it in high school or college, and *The Killing Fields* movie was my first sanitized exposure to the horrors that an entire country had lived through. Even though I had grown up in Ohio, home to the Kent State massacre, on the anniversary of the shootings I would only hear in school that the students were protesting the Vietnam War. Nothing about what had happened in Cambodia. Somehow, I had lived to age 50 without ever knowing that President Nixon had ordered a secret carpet bombing campaign upon neutral Cambodia, a military operation which devastated countless villages and destabilized the country politically. When records on the carpet bombings were declassified in 2000, the true devastation of that secret campaign finally came to light. To put it into perspective, during the entirety of World War II, the Allies dropped 2 million tons of bombs, even including the catastrophic ones which hit Hiroshima and Nagasaki. It is now known that the US dropped 2.7 million tons of bombs onto Cambodia alone, perhaps sadly making it the most bombed country in history.

Leng, like so many in Cambodia still today, grew up in a very vulnerable situation. He said he had no expectation that he could ever have a better life. When he was just 5 years old, his father died from tuberculosis, and he remembers that every responsibility was then placed upon his mom. His family had sold everything they had trying to save his father's life. After the funeral, his mom broke the news to Leng and his siblings that they had nothing left…just $2 to rebuild their lives. He gets emotional speaking about how hard his mother worked trying to make sure they would survive – carrying 100-pound bags of rice on her shoulders and loading ox carts for a tiny bit of income to keep her children fed. Despite their poverty, she insisted her kids stay in school, telling them that only education could change their lives for the better. Now at almost age 70, her injured back is curved and stooped from the heavy loads she carried each day to give her children a better life.

Leng's mom understood suffering all too well. She was one of 12 children in her family and was blessed to have a very loving mother and father. Her dad was well known for his great kindness, and many in their village said she had inherited his gift of sincere warmth and concern for others. Their quiet goodness didn't keep the horrors of the Khmer Rouge from their doorstep, however.

Leng's mom vividly remembers the day that the army came and killed her parents. The soldiers then tied rope around the wrists of all the children, binding their hands behind their backs. They were roughly pushed farther into the jungle, where two soldiers were methodically shooting people. She was made to watch in horror, as all of her siblings were killed in front of her. When it was her turn to have the gun finally aimed at her body, one of the soldiers suddenly recognized her. He said to his partner, "This one is known for her kindness. She's a good person, and I cannot kill her." He quickly cut the ropes from behind her back and let her run free. Somehow, she miraculously hid and survived, but even in her grief she knew she had to do everything she could to help others who were suffering the loss of their families as well.

Leng's mother rescued a lot of people during the war, including one boy whose parents were slaughtered after they had hidden him up in a palm tree. After his mom and dad made sure he had every chance to remain alive, he could only look down in terror as they lost their lives. After the soldiers finished their work and left his parents where they had fallen, he climbed down from his cover and began walking aimlessly. He was filled with so much grief that he wished his own life would end.

When Leng's mother found the boy, his despair touched her kindred heart deeply. She made a promise to him that if he could find it in his heart to trust her, she would now be his family. The boy stayed with Leng's mom for 20 years, even after she married and had children of her own. Because one kind girl took his hand and assured him he didn't have to go on alone, that man is now a teacher in Cambodia who has gone on to educate thousands of students over the years.

This is the mother Leng had the blessing to be raised by. A woman who never wavered in her belief that kindness can change the world. From the time he was a little boy, Leng watched her help others at every opportunity. She taught him that even if someone is poor in circumstances, like their own family, there are so many ways to still give...of one's time, ideas, and compassion. As he grew, his mother's lessons about what is truly important in life took firm hold in Leng's heart as well.

When Leng first moved from his small hometown to the border city of Poipet, he was overwhelmed with the number of children he saw living in hard situations. Cambodia has the highest rate of child labor in Southeast Asia and remains a country plagued by sex trafficking, especially along the border regions. As Leng would walk through the slums and past the casinos, he saw countless children who had no hope of a better future.

Outside the city in the rural villages, he saw kids living without electricity or clean water. He was troubled by the vast numbers of children left completely on their own each day, as adults in the villages (often without documentation) walk long distances into Thailand to work as day laborers in the rice and cassava fields. Far too many kids would go the entire day without food. Without a doubt, the term "vulnerable" sadly applies to tens of thousands of children here.

Leng decided that he couldn't stand by and watch as children in his region were trafficked and abused and growing up illiterate; so, in 2014, he founded a program in the villages outside of Poipet which he called EASEL.

Since so much of our work in Cambodia is tied to education, it's important to have a basic knowledge of the current government system. Public schools in Cambodia are free to attend, but students must provide their own uniforms and books. Classes are often extremely crowded, and children often walk extremely long distances of three miles or more, through jungles and mud, to reach a government school. Because many teachers feel underpaid (earning $250 to $300 per month in 2021), they have created a common, back-door system to earn additional money. They will often withhold key parts of the official curriculum required to pass the national exams, charging families a "tutoring fee" in order to gain access to the full academic materials a child needs. Families living in rural villages or in extreme poverty are often unable to afford even the mandatory uniforms, much less the under-the-table tutoring fees.

According to government reports from 2015, in the region where LWB is working, 36% of eligible children do not attend school. Here's what that looks like in actual numbers: If an estimated 8,000 children enroll in primary school, only 1,000 of those children will complete 6th grade. By 8th grade, that number drops to 250. High school numbers are even more sobering, with only around 50 students each year successfully completing grade 12. Only 14% of high school graduates are girls. Without access to education, these children remain at high risk for exploitation.

Leng's idea back in 2014 was to create a program which would welcome all children who dreamed of having an education. With no outside source of funding, he rented two small rooms and had friends help him build desks from scraps of wood. He went in search of old computers that people would be willing to donate to the center, and very quickly he had hundreds of children wanting to enroll.

For most people living on a shoestring budget, that would have been enough, but Leng knew there were so many other children at risk. When he would ride his motorcycle out to the rural villages surrounding Poipet, he would see throngs of children who were completely unschooled. Knowing it was too far a distance for them to attend his EASEL program, he came up with the wonderful idea of gathering high school teens together to encourage them to change their community for the better. Soon after, MERCY (Mobile Education through Remarkable Cycling Youth) was born. Each weekend, the MERCY teens would pile two to three across on their bicycles and ride several miles out to remote villages. This was often easier said than done, as the monsoon season would turn the small dirt roads to each village into often impassable mud. Still, they persisted, and for the very first time, children in those villages not only had story time and a chance to learn the basics of reading, they also had important lessons on hygiene and needing to be wary of strangers.

As word spread of the great work that Leng was doing for children in the region, a sea of families began contacting him to please help their children as well. It was a heavy burden for a young man who struggles to ever say no to someone in need.

As we sat and listened to Leng tell us about all he had already accomplished, he then asked if we were ready to begin our visits to the villages. It was then that I got my very first ride on a Cambodian tuk-

tuk, still my favorite way to get around. These motorcycle-pulled "carriages" offer great views of the local countryside, and the sudden bumps and jolts that come from hitting giant ruts on dirt roads are a very quick way of getting to know your fellow seat mates better!

As we made the journey out to the first village Leng wanted us to visit, he told us he needed to quickly stop and check on a girl who was sick. He explained that two years earlier, Christine had been diagnosed with tuberculosis, the same disease which had taken his father's life. You probably already know TB is a bacterial infection that primarily affects the lungs. What you might not know is that at one point, the United Nations announced that TB would be eliminated in the world by 2025 as doctors had become so skilled in treating it. However, in the late 1980s, TB infections began to rise once again, and tuberculosis was declared a global emergency. Conventional TB is easily treatable and has a 90% cure rate if managed correctly. Without proper treatment, however, two-thirds of people who contract tuberculosis will die — a staggering one million people each year.

We climbed down from the tuk-tuk and made our way into the jungle. This was my very first visit to a Cambodian family's home, and I will never forget how kind they were when we arrived, quickly bringing stools for us to sit upon. Most homes in this area are simple square structures made from wood or metal sheeting, built up on stilts so the monsoonal rain and flooding won't impact the living area. It was a very peaceful setting, and, as I took in the cloth hammocks tied to the trees, I did not immediately see Christine. Then my eyes settled on a young lady who was very, very ill. She was so painfully thin that her entire being seemed fragile. I could see every bone in her body, and I held my breath as her family began to tell her story.

When their daughter first became sick, they did everything they could to help her, even selling off most of their land and possessions in order to get her medical care. Yet another sad result from the Khmer Rouge tragedy is that some believe only 45 medical doctors in the entirety of Cambodia survived the bloodshed, and 20 of those then left the country. For this reason, access to quality health care, especially in the rural regions far from the capital city of Phnom

Penh, is quite limited even today. Despite spending all their funds searching for local treatment, Christine had not regained her health. With no money left for additional medical care, her parents and siblings had to watch her become even more frail.

As I sat with Christine that day, she was breathing only with the help of oxygen. Her family tried desperately to provide her with a constant supply, but the $10 required every three days to refill the canister was well beyond their means. Leng had been helping them out whenever he could. We had stopped that day so he could give them a few dollars more for Christine to continue to breathe. He shared with us that Christine had to drop out of school because of her illness. It was painful to look into her eyes as he told the story because there was just so much sadness over what she had lost. She had been an excellent student before her illness robbed her of the learning that she dearly loved.

Christine wasn't the only member of the family whose education had been cut short because of her battle with TB. Her brother Paul, a senior in high school when Christine was diagnosed with tuberculosis, decided to sacrifice his own future in order to help pay for medical treatment for the sister he loved. Paul dropped out of high school and crossed the border into Thailand to search for work. He was single-minded in his goal to send money back home to try and save Christine's life. He later told us, "Every day I worked in Thailand with the hope that one day my sister will be better. I dreamed of the day that she and I would return to school and study together once again."

As I locked eyes once more with Christine, I kept praying that we weren't too late. This devoted family had given everything they had to save her life. I knew we had to get her to the capital city to see an infectious disease specialist, but that was more than a seven-hour drive from where we were sitting. I didn't see how she would ever make the journey when she was so very weak.

Through the work I do, there are times that I get to experience the greatest joys, such as seeing a child's heart healed or knowing an orphaned child has been chosen by a permanent family. There are times of great sorrow as well, when a child we have been trying to help passes away or when we see children living in such hard places. But there are also times that I feel just completely unworthy to be part of the very emotional moments our work often entails, and I had one of those moments when Leng told Christine and her family that we would pay all the costs for her to go to the best hospital possible. Christine began to silently cry, followed by her family and then Leng. We sat on little stools in the dirt in complete silence, tears streaming down each person's face, as I watched hope slowly come back into their hearts.

I can't fully describe what I was feeling inside, but it seemed too private and emotional a moment for me as a complete stranger to share with Christine's family. There was a feeling of shame in my heart knowing that most likely just a few hundred dollars was what had stopped this incredibly gentle and beautiful girl from having a full evaluation and correct treatment done. But, of course, we were going to do all we could to give her that chance.

We arranged for a special ambulance to carry Christine and her father to Phnom Penh, so that she could have the oxygen she needed to breathe during the trip. After doctors there examined her, they determined that she had a very resistant strain of TB, which is why she was still struggling. The initial plan was for her to undergo eight months of strong medication that would not be easy on her frail body.

As she began her first treatments, we all prayed that Christine would finally respond to the proper regimen. It is heartbreaking to remember just how hard she fought to get well. Her body was just too depleted by that time. Eating soon became a challenge, and then even trying to sit up or raise her head became difficult. Just ten weeks after we had sat together at her home, Christine closed her eyes for the final time. Her tight-knit family was devastated. They had given everything they had, with such unlimited love, and now their precious daughter was gone.

When I think back on that enormous loss, I still get emotional. Christine was the first child I met in Cambodia, but we were unable to save her life. The only comfort we can take is in remembering her beautiful spirit and vowing to work even harder to make sure no other child in our programs ever loses their life to a treatable condition.

I also look back with gratitude for our supporters, who went on to help us build a successful scholarship program in Cambodia, to assist rural families like Christine's who could never afford the cost of a college education. In fact, one of the first scholarship recipients was Christine's devoted brother, Paul. Shortly after her funeral, he shared with Leng that he dreamed of someday rising above their impoverished circumstances. Despite dropping out of high school to help his sister, Paul still longed to attend university. He knew it was impossible though due to the family's financial situation.

Leng encouraged Paul to go ahead and sit for the high school completion exam, even though he had never finished his senior year. We didn't want the door to higher education to be permanently shut for him. Paul is an incredibly intelligent young man, and we were overjoyed when he passed the examinations needed to apply for college.

In 2017, Paul became one of our first scholarship recipients. He was accepted into the electrical engineering program at the National Polytechnic Institute of Cambodia. He is an exceptional student. He carries a course load of nine to ten classes per semester, even during COVID, and never complains despite the challenges. He says that the LWB scholarship program changed his life, and he thanks those "who believe in children like me, who otherwise have no possibility of ever going to university."

I know Christine would be so proud of her brother. He was willing to surrender everything for his love of family. Now, with his sister's memory carried deeply in his heart, he will soon finish college and take the next big step into his future. I have no doubt that he's going to continue making a difference in the world. He'll be an amazing role model for the next generation to come.

When I think of both Leng's and Christine's families, the word "sacrifice" comes to mind. Without any hesitation, they were willing to give up what they valued for the sake of helping others. Leng's mother did back-breaking work each day to make sure her children could be educated. Paul had given up his own dream of finishing school so his sister would have a chance at receiving medical care.

When you think about that powerful word, what does it mean in your own life? Have you ever given up something you wanted dearly to help someone else instead? Through my work with LWB, I've seen firsthand how sacrifice is a cornerstone of a strong community. Selflessly giving to others creates bonds that are hard to break. We only need to look at the medical workers who have stepped forward during this awful COVID pandemic to feel the communal spirit our world has now in praying for those on the front lines.

The beautiful thing about sacrifice, however, is that it doesn't always have to be bold and grand. It can be quiet…simply choosing to help wherever we can. In a world that promotes the message that each of us somehow deserves to "have it all," I believe stepping forward to help those in need remains a vital part of our humanity. And when those around us see even simple sacrifices being made for a common good, that's when the first stirrings of authentic community begin to take hold.

The Heart of Community

Chapter 2: Trust

Trust is an important and tender aspect of all relationships because it requires us to be both vulnerable and courageous.

Vijohn Chea, LWB-Cambodia Education Manager

"Please prepare for mud."

These were the four words I received in an email from Leng as I finalized my plans to visit Cambodia for the first time. I had traveled extensively through rural villages in China over the last decade; so I have to admit that those wise words went in and out of my brain far too quickly in the rush to finalize plane tickets and visa requirements.

I should have paid much more attention in school to what "monsoonal rain" really means.

On our first full day in Cambodia, we climbed on board a tuk-tuk to begin our trip out to Sokhem Village, a remote location home to around 170 children. Sokhem Village had been established following the war with the Khmer Rouge as a place where people who had lost their limbs from fighting or land mines could settle. Leng told us the village was still just a single lane of mostly stilt houses and that his heart was burdened by the number of vulnerable children there.

The rain was pouring down in solid sheets as we left Poipet, and our kind moto driver was already soaked to the core. He shouted over the roar of the storm that we needed to stop for gas along the way. He pulled up to a roadside cart, where I quickly learned that the yellow liquid stored in dozens of old soda bottles was definitely not Mountain Dew. An elderly woman hurried over with a plastic funnel and quickly poured gasoline from the glass bottle into the motorcycle tank.

On our way once again, we soon turned off the paved streets of the city onto a dirt road, with the skies continuing to deluge the ground with rain. Leng told us it was about seven miles out to Sokhem, and it quickly became clear why so many villages in Cambodia are completely cut off during monsoon season. As the dirt road turned into ever deepening mud, our tuk-tuk became stuck several times. As the driver revved the tuk-tuk engine trying to get us free, its futilely spinning wheels caused us to sink further. We would climb out to push it free, only to go a short distance and become mired in the mud once again. When we were still a few miles from the village, the small motorcycle engine on the tuk-tuk finally overheated, and we assured the driver we didn't mind walking the rest of the way to the village.

We all started in our sandals, but soon the mud swiftly reached mid-calf. After having our shoes get sucked off in the deep ooze repeatedly, we finally admitted defeat and journeyed forward in our bare feet.

It was a lot more slippery than it looked. I have to admit I was laughing inside that I had decided to wear a long black skirt to meet the local villagers, as I had wanted to make a good first impression. I have a photo from that rainy walk that always makes me smile. Leng had completely wiped out at one point, falling straight on his back into what was now a pond of clay instead of a road. By the time we finally saw the first few houses in the village come into view, the rest of us were covered in mud from head to toe as well. Several of the kids ran out to meet us and tried to hold back giggles as they came up to study the foreigners' legs and feet, which were now a glorious, gloopy brown.

Needless to say, none of that mattered as I looked around at all the wonderful children who were saying hello to us. Leng had already briefed us on some of the immense challenges that the children in Sokhem Village faced each day. The first thing that struck me was the number of kids who were clearly undernourished. I'd start talking with a child I thought was around age 5 or 6, only to be told that they were actually 10 or 12. At one point I even naively asked Leng whether it was a cultural practice in the village to dye a child's hair blonde, because so many of the little ones around us had hair that was a brittle yellow or light orange. I now know that many of the children in Sokhem had Kwashiorkor malnutrition, which is caused by a lack of protein in the diet. Protein is essential for a child's body to repair and make new cells; without it, growth shuts down. One of the common signs of Kwashiorkor in Africa and Southeast Asia is when a child's once normally black hair turns brittle and blonde. While my hair color might have come from a bottle, theirs tragically had not.

In China, I had seen far too many children in orphanages struggle to gain weight. With overworked nannies not having enough hands to hold all the babies, it was common to roll up a small towel and prop a bottle next to an infant's mouth in an attempt to have them self-feed. It rarely worked well, as most of the formula would pour out onto the crib instead of into the struggling baby's mouth. We had taken in hundreds of failure-to-thrive children to our specialized healing homes in China and celebrated every pound they would gain once they were fed by hand. This was the first time, however, that I had seen an entire village of children who were so clearly stunted in their growth. In fact, the first heights and weights we gathered showed over 75% of them were suffering from chronic malnutrition.

Children with this condition, of course, develop much more slowly physically and are far more vulnerable to disease. Chronic malnutrition can have a devastating effect on a child's cognitive abilities as well. With a persistent lack of vital nutrients, a child's brain can develop memory troubles and learning disabilities. In a nutshell, lack of food as a child can lead to long-term health and intellectual issues as an adult. I worried for every undersized child I saw.

As we began discussing the children's educational status in Sokhem Village, I learned that out of the 170 children there, only around eight had been to formal school. As I mentioned previously, the border region between Cambodia and Thailand is known for human trafficking, and horrifically even young children can be taken for forced labor and sex crimes. Everyone in the villages knows at least one person who has fallen victim. For many families living in remote regions, it is just too dangerous for their children to walk the three to ten miles each way to the closest government school, and so the children simply stay put.

In addition, in many villages along the border, a majority of adults leave early each morning to cross into Thailand to search for day labor. They return home late in the evening, which means a high percentage of children in the villages are all on their own each day, fending for themselves. These "left behind" children are ripe for exploitation. Growing up without access to education perpetuates the cycle of poverty for an entire new generation.

One of the first little girls I met in Sokhem Village was 9-year-old Debra. She had watched us come up the path while holding her naked and clearly malnourished baby brother on her hip. His abdomen was distended, and his head seemed too big for his little body. Debra's slight build and straw-colored hair were outward signs that she wasn't getting enough to eat as well. Debra was in charge of all three of her little brothers, as her father had abandoned them to start a new family, and her mother would disappear frequently into Thailand for long periods of time. While I was still trying to process that a 9-year-old was the primary caregiver in the family, I quickly saw that there were lots of other young girls holding babies on their backs or hips as well. In this rural region of Cambodia, children often take on the role of mama, while their own mothers leave for work in Thailand.

Debra led us to one of the small village homes, made of sheets of corrugated metal and wood. Inside, Leng had set up a small school program so the children in Sokhem could learn to read. In front of us were about 30 of the village children, sitting on a green plastic tarp that had been laid on the dirt floor. There was a small whiteboard hung on some bamboo sticks that all their eyes were fixed upon. This one little room had children of every age inside, from toddlers to adolescents, but everyone was listening intently to the young teen who was teaching, eagerly soaking up the Khmer characters on the board.

We sat quietly and watched the lesson, quickly realizing that by partnering with this village, we could make an enormous difference in the children's nutritional and educational needs. As we returned to Poipet later that day, we excitedly brainstormed with Leng on ways to make a tangible difference in their lives.

I shared with him the success LWB had found inside Chinese orphanages, creating "Believe in Me" schools so that all children, regardless of their abilities, could have access to learning. Despite the clear differences between a Chinese welfare institute and a Cambodian village, the need was very much the same. All children have a right to education. We already had the experience of setting up schools inside orphanages; so, if it was too dangerous for the kids in Sokhem to make the long journey to the government school each day, why couldn't we bring a comprehensive school program to the very heart of their village as well?

These are the kinds of dreams that get my heart pounding with enthusiasm, and I couldn't wait to work with Leng and our team to develop a formal proposal. I was soon to learn, however, that one of the most essential components of any true partnership was going to be a lot more difficult than expected in this region. No authentic community can be built without trust, and the people in the remote villages along the border had very good reasons to doubt even our best intentions.

Whenever I think of trust, my mind immediately goes to my great grandmother's antique teacup, which I have sitting up high on a shelf in my kitchen. It's a special treasure to me as it has now been handed down in our family for four generations. As a child, I was fascinated with its fragile porcelain, painted with rose flowers and miniature green leaves. When it was finally given to me after becoming a mom myself, I hid it away in a drawer out of the sight of my rambunctious, tumbleweed boys.

I remember taking it out of the hutch one day to show to a dear friend. As she held the delicate handle, she said, "Isn't this the perfect analogy for trust? It's impossible to put a value on this tiny cup, because it means so much to your family and can never be replaced. But in one swift second you could drop it, shattering it across the floor." She continued, "And while you could work really, really hard to put all the pieces back together, and perhaps with enough time even repair the cracks to be almost invisible to the naked eye, the reality is that it can never be as perfect and strong as it is right at this moment... when it's whole."

I agreed it was indeed a wonderful symbol for trust in relationships, and she then looked at me and said, "Amy, as we go through our lives and set an example for our children, we need to do everything possible to **not drop the cup.**"

I've thought about that conversation many times over the years, especially as our extraordinary work helping orphaned and rural children has unfolded. Trust is an integral part of everything we do with LWB. There is trust on the part of orphanages when they allow us to move a child into our care. There is trust on the part of the children and their caregivers, when we arrange for life-changing surgeries or encourage them to set big goals for their futures. And of course, in innumerable ways, there is the precious trust of our donors…trust that when we take in a kind person's hard-earned dollars, we will be the absolute best stewards of those funds we can be.

I never take that trust for granted. I have a phrase I use with our teams that they are probably sick of hearing: LWB must have **unimpeachable ethics**. Each and every time we consider a new project or evaluate the success of the programs we are running, we must ask ourselves how to make the biggest impact possible for the children, while conducting our work with the highest honesty and integrity. In other words, we cannot "drop the cup." There are just too many vulnerable children who depend on us now; so the trust we build in the LWB community must always be nurtured and protected.

The people living in Sokhem Village, however, didn't know the first thing about LWB's commitment to children when we came walking down their dirt road caked in mud. It's hard to trust when all you have from the past are reasons why you shouldn't. I soon learned that we were far from the first NGO to arrive in the border villages promising aid. In fact, a stream of fly-by-night "charity workers" had come through over the years, posing thin and dusty children in front of the most run-down structures they could find. These visitors would frantically snap photos of the kids and promise them all a better future, only to disappear with their "poverty porn" pictures, never to be heard from again.

The people in these remote regions had been promised access to water and electricity, free school for their children, and well-paid jobs. No one ever followed through. In the worst situations, strangers even convinced some of the illiterate and unknowing families that they could provide girls in the village with wonderful jobs in cities such as Bangkok. They were told the girls would work in offices or private homes, allowing their daughters to send critical funds back to the village. It was only when yet another girl would somehow escape from forced prostitution and arrive back home in shame that the horrific truth of empty promises would become known.

The village leaders had every right to doubt our "we really want to help" words. We had our work cut out for us, but we were ready to get started building those essential seeds of trust. There were 170 children in the village in real need of assistance, and we were determined to show the Sokhem leaders that one of the fundamental principles at LWB is that we follow through on what we say. Of course, we all know the old adage that actions speak louder than words; so, as soon as the funds were in place, Leng returned to the village to purchase a plot of land big enough for a school. I hoped this first major action would speak the truth that when it came to the vulnerable children of Sokhem Village, we were in this for the long haul.

Within just a few weeks, our first Believe in Me school in Cambodia was ready for construction. We had planned a simple, three-room schoolhouse, and the children of Sokhem were beyond excited that a primary school would soon be right in their village. Leng would send daily videos and photos from the site. The first images we received were of the kids gathering rocks from the land, hoisting them up in a contest to see who had found the biggest one. They all had huge smiles on their faces. Even the toddlers had little wooden buckets, picking up pebbles from the dirt and walking them over to the plot of land we had purchased.

In a region known for child labor, though, I immediately went into panic mode. I called Leng, saying, "We can't have the children doing any part of the construction work!" He chuckled and quietly told me to relax, while explaining that it was only for the one afternoon. He wanted every child in the village to put their hands on this life-changing project. By gathering stones to lay a strong foundation, they could claim ownership of the school and always know they played a part in making it a reality. For the rest of the construction time, the kids just played on the giant dirt piles outside (a universal love of children around the world), while the real builders put up the walls and roof.

In December 2016, we opened our first LWB-Cambodia school, welcoming every school-aged child in the village. Reading their intake forms was quite sobering, with many children telling our team how lonely they felt all day being left completely on their own. Far too many had also innocently stated, *"My siblings and I have no food to eat at home."*

One of the first little girls enrolled was 10-year-old Lucy. She was one of the children whose age I had guessed so incorrectly on that first trip, as she was only the size of a small 5-year-old. Her mom had tragically passed away earlier that year, leaving seven small children behind. Lucy's father was an alcoholic who would frequently disappear for days on end, leaving this little girl to fend for herself and her siblings. She was always torn between wanting her father to return and not. While he might sometimes bring back a small amount of food for the children's hungry tummies, more often he just brought back his anger and forceful slaps if she ever got in his way.

Lucy was beyond excited about the chance to go to school. She had come to the construction site every morning to count down the days until it opened. She was also there the day we prepared to hoist up the metal sign which read "LWB Kitchen House." To begin battling the chronic malnutrition in the village, we had added an outdoor cafeteria and kitchen to the school property. To ensure that more adults would be present in the village each day as well, we hired several widows to become official LWB cooks. Each day, these "kitchen ladies" would prepare a delicious hot lunch for the students.

Lucy looked at the kitchen house sign in front of her with joy, an image that was captured forever in a photo showing the biggest smile on her face. I can't imagine what a relief it must have been for her to know there would be food available to her each day at school. No longer would she have to gather grass and weeds from the field to try and stem her hunger.

A few months after our hot lunch program in Sokhem began, Lucy told us shyly that she eats as much as she possibly can during lunchtime, because she never knows whether she will get dinner that night or breakfast the next morning. Now, whether or not her often absent father provides her with rice to cook each week, she takes comfort in knowing that a hot, nutritious lunch will always be waiting for her. Consistency leads to trust, doesn't it? It's built in even the smallest moments when we regularly show up for each other.

I also think of the word *trust* when I remember a little boy in China whose life was only saved because our director there never stopped trying to earn trust with one particular orphanage. We had wanted to gain access to the children in this facility for years, after a little girl who was clearly malnourished showed up on an adoption waiting list. The adoption agency who received her file contacted us with concern, wondering if we could possibly visit the institution to see how the little girl was faring.

Despite having good relationships with many of the orphanages in her province, each time we would ask to visit we were given an adamant "no." Ming kept trying, however, phoning every so often to check on the little girl's status and let them know we were available for any pressing needs. Then suddenly, after four long years of requests, the yes we'd been hoping for finally came. We were invited to visit the orphanage and meet the children in person.

In June 2020, our director walked into the small orphanage and came face to face with a young boy named Ollie. He was lying flat on his back in a metal crib, with his legs drawn up like a little frog because having them straight caused him pain. He had been born with a medical condition known as anal atresia, a birth defect where the rectum and part of the intestine are malformed. It makes it very difficult for a child to pass stool, which I know a lot of people aren't comfortable talking about, despite it being an essential part of every human's life. If anal atresia is not corrected surgically, signs of distal bowel obstruction soon develop as the child is fed.

In many parts of China, especially the rural regions, anal atresia is seen as a sign of being cursed. For this reason, many children born with this condition find themselves abandoned. Such was the case for Ollie, and, because he was taken to an orphanage with limited medical care, the urgent surgery he needed at birth was never done.

For two years, his tiny body couldn't work the way it should, so eating and even moving became increasingly painful. Ollie learned to lie quietly in his orphanage crib all day, assuming the frog leg position to try and ease the constant and often severe discomfort he now felt throughout his body.

Thankfully, our healing home director has helped countless children born with this special need. When he placed his hands on Ollie's hard and distended belly, he knew that the little boy needed urgent medical care right away. He carefully picked up Ollie in his arms and held the little boy gently the entire way to the hospital. He told us that Ollie was too timid to look him in the eyes and didn't like to be touched, most likely because it made his abdomen hurt even more.

Ollie was admitted immediately to the hospital, where doctors began emergency treatment. The CT scans sent to us were heartbreaking, as two years of build-up had caused extensive damage to Ollie's intestines. The surgeon explained that the little boy had been found just in the nick of time.

Ollie underwent several weeks of agonizing treatments to prepare his body for a major bowel resection and colostomy. Thankfully, an incredibly special LWB nanny had arrived at the hospital. She was able to hold Ollie tenderly in her arms and whisper he would soon be okay.

When the moms and dads on the hospital ward learned about little Ollie and what he had already endured in his short life, their hearts were filled with compassion. They showered him with kindness so he could know that despite being orphaned, he had lots of people who cared. When they saw that he didn't have the ability to support his lower body, after lying in an orphanage crib for two years, the determined moms began lifting him up each day to stretch his legs. They told him repeatedly what a special little boy he was.

Just one short week after his admittance to the hospital, Ollie had already made enormous progress. He was finally able to drink a tiny bit of formula, and the pain in his tummy began to decrease as his intestines were cleared. Even better, he quickly learned to sit up on his own for a few minutes at a time, thanks to the encouragement from his new friends on the ward. He really enjoyed having a new view of the world versus lying flat on his back in a crib. The most beautiful sign of hope arrived when Ollie's first tiny smile finally broke free. By the time his surgery was completed, and he was released from the hospital to stay at our healing home, the security and love he now felt turned those adorable grins into full-out laughter.

We know there is a lot of physical and emotional hurt that he will still need to overcome, but we give thanks that he is right where he needs to be. We're grateful that his orphanage finally felt they could trust us to make that all-important first visit. We hope trust continues to grow so that many more children like Ollie will receive the medical care they need.

Even among those to whom we are closest, new situations can sometimes arise in which we must choose whether or not to trust. Thankfully, with open and honest communication, our reinforced faith in each other can lead to remarkable outcomes.

One of our key directors in China is a man named Ming. He and I first met all the way back in 2004, when LWB decided to begin foster care for orphaned children in his province. Since that time, he has become like a brother to me. We have traveled throughout China together, even facing white-out blizzards and near-death accidents. He has been by my side as we've rushed newborn babies to the hospital and dreamed of even bigger ways to get more help to the children. Despite all our history together, however, there was one child's case that made us discuss the vital importance of trust once again.

LWB's Unity Initiative in China provides surgeries to children living in extreme poverty. Many of the children who end up in Chinese orphanages have medical needs well beyond their parents' ability to fund care. In some tragic cases, the most vulnerable are left to the state's care after their desperate families realize they could never provide their children with the medical care they need. Our Unity program is one of our many efforts to help keep families together. By providing surgeries to correct issues such as cleft and heart defects, we can prevent some children from ever being abandoned in the first place.

In December 2017, Ming met 1-year-old Kyle. Many of our Unity surgeries at that time were being done at a heart hospital where Kyle's mom had just brought her son. Ming had gone to check on several children LWB was helping with surgery and saw the distraught mother crying in the hallway. When he went to ask if she needed assistance, she told him that she had just been told yet again that nothing could be done to save the life of her little boy.

Kyle had been her miracle baby. He was conceived after eight difficult years of infertility, and the surprise of the pregnancy they had longed for brought great joy to the entire family. They began counting down the days until their sweet child would be born.

Baby Kyle had no desire to leave his mama's womb, however, and after ten months of pregnancy, he finally came into the world by cesarean delivery. As the whole family was still immersed in the excitement of his birth, Kyle remained listless and floppy. At four days old, he was found to have an extremely complex heart defect, as well as Down syndrome. The news caused his elderly grandfather to collapse with grief.

Kyle's mom was completely committed to her son, and she refused to listen to the local doctor who told her she should just take her baby home to die. Despite their extreme poverty, she knew she had to find a hospital willing to help her son. Over the next year, she made several journeys to top children's hospitals in their region, finally going all the way to Shanghai. Each time, she received the same sobering advice: "Your son has Down syndrome. He struggles to breathe and continually falls ill. You should take the child back to your village and let nature take its course."

On the day that Ming first met Kyle's mom, she had just received the same advice from yet another surgeon. She told Ming through her tears that she knew she had to come to terms with the reality that her precious child's heart would soon fail, but her own heart was absolutely broken when she thought of losing him. In the photo we have of Kyle and his mom from that day, there is so much sorrow in her eyes. Kyle looks weak and tired, with his lips a deep blue from his continual lack of oxygen.

When we first heard the story of little Kyle, we knew there was an incredible hospital the mom had not yet visited. The Children's Hospital of Fudan University in Shanghai has some of the best cardiac surgeons in the world. If anyone could help Kyle in China, we knew it would be their surgeons. We asked Ming if he could call the mom to get Kyle's medical records so we could send them to Fudan for another opinion.

When he called their home, Kyle's mom answered the phone already crying. She was shattered with grief, knowing she shouldn't give up on her son but also knowing they had already sunk heavily into debt trying to find a hospital who could help. She agreed to send us the echo scans of Kyle's heart, and we quickly forwarded them on to Fudan for their thoughts. They replied within hours that his heart appeared so complex that only a cardiac catheterization could determine if he was operable. The next step seemed simple… let's get Kyle to Shanghai so the cath procedure could be done.

This was the moment when Ming paused. We had moved away from sending many children to Fudan because rising medical costs in China had put the cost of heart surgery there well beyond what we normally raised per child. If Kyle actually had a chance at healing, without a doubt, his surgery would be an extremely expensive one due to the complexity of his little heart.

It was easy for me to say, "Please call the family," but Ming had been the one standing in the hospital hallway watching a weary mom break down in tears. He had been the one who listened to her anguished sobs over the phone. And so, with a deep breath he felt he had to ask, "Before I make this call to the family to let them know Fudan wants to do another exam, I want to make sure LWB is fully committed to sponsoring the necessary surgeries if Kyle is operable. This family is extremely impoverished, simple farmers of corn and wheat. They are in such deep pain already but have begun trying to come to terms with their son not having long to live. I can't give them hope only to take it away once again if the operation costs are too high for us to cover."

Without a doubt, I knew the medical costs would be high, but I also knew that the LWB community genuinely believes in our motto that "Every Child Counts." While some doctors might have looked at Kyle and felt his life wasn't as valuable because of Down syndrome, our supporters continually wrap their arms around those with special needs. It is one of our core values that EVERY child deserves both dignity and love, and those in our community share that vision as well. It's for that very reason that I trust our supporters will join with us when a child like Kyle comes into our hands. It's because of that trust that I didn't hesitate for a second when asking Ming to go ahead and make the call. "I promise if that little boy is operable, LWB will see him through somehow."

Just four days later, Kyle and his mom arrived in Shanghai. They had taken the overnight train, arriving at 6:30 in the morning. Mom looked so exhausted. Kyle's dark lips confirmed what the intake nurse quickly discovered. His oxygen levels were at a critically low 70%.

The heart surgeon arranged for an immediate cath, which showed that Kyle had Double Outlet Right Ventricle, a rare congenital heart defect. With DORV, the heart's two major arteries (the pulmonary and aorta) both connect to the right ventricle. In a normal heart, the pulmonary artery connects to the right ventricle, and the aorta connects to the left. DORV creates a serious problem for a baby because the blood circulating through the body doesn't have enough oxygen. In the US, this condition is often repaired a few days after birth and almost always by a few months of age. Kyle had struggled for 20 long months to get the oxygen he needed, and his heart was beginning to fail. Surgery would need to be done as quickly as possible to give him any chance at life.

His mom texted our team with a string of thoughts that very evening:

> *Sorry to disturb you. I know it's late. You should get some rest. Good night. Good night. We are so poor. There's no more way to make money. It's so very hard. But I feel so fulfilled with the news that my son might be saved. But the doctor said surgery cannot wait. Without surgery...*

There the text ended, as the enormity of both renewed hope mixed with anxious worry flooded her mind once again.

We sent out an immediate appeal to raise the funds that Kyle needed for his surgery, and the outpouring of support for this beautiful little boy was incredible to see. The funds were raised in less than a week. Soon after, Kyle was wheeled into the OR to undergo a seven-hour operation to reroute the arteries of his heart.

In an ideal recovery, a child will be weaned from the mechanical ventilator that helps them breathe during surgery within 24 hours. We normally don't worry if it takes 48 to 96 hours for a child to come off the vent, but anything much longer than that begins to be a concern. Doctors start to wonder whether a child whose pulmonary circulation has been switched through surgery will ever be able to breathe again on their own.

Kyle was unable to be weaned from the ventilator. Three days turned into two weeks, and only the machine kept his lungs filling with oxygen. Fluid began to build up around his lungs, and the medical team started warning us that Kyle could pass away. The heart surgeon carefully explained to Kyle's mom the grim reality her son might be facing, but he remained hopeful that perhaps Kyle just needed more time to finally turn the corner. She just kept saying how grateful she was to the doctors and everyone with LWB who had given to make his surgery possible.

Another week went by, and Kyle was still connected to the vent. We then got the awful news that he had developed chylothorax, a rare but serious condition in which milky lymph (chyle) formed in the digestive system accumulates in the chest cavity and makes it even harder to breathe. We rushed to get him a specialized formula that could possibly help with his recovery. Synthetic formula in China is extremely expensive, however, and doctors said Kyle might need to stay on it for quite some time.

When she heard the news, Kyle's mom insisted on working a few hours a day in the hospital cafeteria to contribute to his formula fund. Even though we assured her that we would cover all the costs, she told us we needed to save those funds for other children needing surgery like her son. She told our manager, "I will find a way to get his formula. It is my responsibility as his mom."

Five weeks after Kyle underwent his open-heart operation, he was finally able to take those important first breaths on his own. While he would need to stay almost another month in the hospital recovering from his complications, on the day Kyle and his mom boarded the train in Shanghai to return to their small village, Kyle's oxygen levels were a wonderfully normal 95%.

Over the next year, we continued to send shipments of the specialty formula Kyle needed to their home. (You surely didn't think we'd let his mom go more into debt from those costs, did you?) Each update we received on Kyle was even better. With his new strength and energy, he gradually learned to toddle around on his own and soon was laughing and babbling away.

His mom is so proud of her little boy and tells us that Kyle brings so much fun and joy to their lives with his sunny disposition. It is wonderful to know that yet another beautiful family gets to stay united, because of the sacred gift of trust. Trust in the doctors, trust between our team, and trust within the entire LWB circle. It's the essential ingredient that every community needs to thrive, as it gives room for bigger dreams, greater love, and the most remarkable possibilities.

For all the little Kyles who still need someone to believe in them, and for kids like Lucy and Ollie…we simply can't drop the cup. When you make a promise to help a hurting child, trust cannot be broken.

Chapter 3: Commitment

Commitment arises from love.

Kim Eng, LWB-Cambodia Foster Parent

Love Without Boundaries has established foster care programs in every country where we work, providing full-time care for children who have been orphaned, relinquished, or severely abused. We began our foster care program in China, back when a majority of orphanages were overcrowded and understaffed. It was not uncommon for infants to spend almost every moment of their lives in institutional care confined to a crib, lying flat on their backs looking up at the ceiling. As we would walk through the baby rooms of orphanages, especially in those with limited resources, we would be met by the solemn, silent gazes of children who had learned that their cries would not be answered. It was haunting... heartbreaking... and it didn't require a psychology dissertation to understand viscerally that babies need parents.

As I wrote in *The Heart of an Orphan*, however, I was terrified to consider foster care, as the projects we were doing up to that point in orphanages were primarily one-time needs, such as arranging for a heart or cleft surgery. Progressing into the foster care realm would require an absolute full-time commitment to a child, as there was no way we could move a baby out of an orphanage, give them a mom or dad of their very own, and then change our minds.

It was the right thing to do, though. Children deserve families, not institutions, and so we opened our first foster care program in China in 2004, moving children abandoned with medical needs into caring homes in the local community. Over the next decade, we expanded foster care in China to 22 different locations and helped over 3,500 children receive family-based care. It was an amazing, deeply impactful program. As the children in our foster homes would go on to be adopted, both domestically and internationally, we would regularly hear from their new parents that the emotional attachments they had formed in our care had made such a difference in their ability to bond with their new forever families. Love poured into a child from the earliest moments possible was a gift that would last a lifetime.

When LWB expanded our work to Cambodia in 2016, we originally weren't planning to implement foster care, as the situation there with orphanages is a lot different than in China. Throughout mainland China, most children who end up in institutional care do not fit the dictionary definition of orphan, "a child whose parents have died." Instead, they arrive into orphanage care through secret abandonment, since it's still considered a crime in most provinces to relinquish a child. Almost all of these children, over 98%, are born with medical needs. These children are mostly placed into official, government funded institutions, and the birth parents usually remain hidden and unknown.

Google "Cambodia + orphans," however, and you will see abundant newspaper articles and studies about the large number of orphanages that have been set up for profit and house children who have known, living family members. In Cambodia, only a small percentage of children fit the standard definition of orphan as well, but the main reason children end up in orphanage care is poverty. Their parents cannot afford to even feed themselves, much less provide food to their children.

I'll admit that when we first made the decision to expand our programs to Cambodia, I wanted absolutely nothing to do with the orphanages there since the system is so murky. Most of the hundreds of orphanages that have been set up in the last decade are based in Phnom Penh and Siem Reap, high tourism cities where throngs of visitors (or voluntourists) cycle through to come and play with the kids and then go home. International adoptions from Cambodia had been stopped in 2001 due to a high level of corruption and greed, but that didn't stop unscrupulous people from realizing that "orphan care" could still be a highly lucrative business. I wanted no part of that.

While our first project in Cambodia was to build an elementary school for the children in rural Sokhem Village, we very quickly had to face the reality that there were orphaned and abandoned children in this region who were living in extremely unprotected situations. There is no government orphanage along the western border; so Leng, LWB-Cambodia's director, began receiving phone calls from the police and local village leaders asking if LWB could possibly care for children whose parents had died or who'd been left completely on their own when their parents migrated to Thailand without them. It's impossible to look the other way when you are getting photos of a 3-year-old scavenging for food in dumpsters or when a 1-week-old baby is left all alone at our school.

I soon learned that most of the NGO shelters in the Poipet region will only accept children ages 5 and up, leaving babies and toddlers especially vulnerable. They are often sent to the larger cities in Cambodia to enter the orphanage system, which few then are ever able to leave. With our knowledge of implementing well monitored foster care in China, we decided it was time to get government permission to expand this program to Cambodia, knowing full well that we'd have to build it from the ground up and face a whole new set of challenges.

Our foster care model in China involved partnering with local governments on foster family support, with LWB providing half of a foster parent's monthly stipend and the local civil affairs department providing the remaining half. The orphanage retained legal guardianship of the children in our care; so, ultimately, the final decisions regarding a child's future rested in the hands of each individual orphanage director.

Cambodia, on the other hand, offers no government financial assistance for family-based care. A severe lack of social workers in the country and an overworked welfare system means that the funding and case management for foster care falls directly on individual charities. We are also given full legal guardianship of the children in our care, which means, when we accept a child into foster care in Cambodia, we're making a long-term commitment, to adulthood in many cases. We are fully responsible for the child's health, education, and well-being. Essentially, we become the child's legal parents, and it is up to us to ensure that each individual child has the most promising future possible. Excuse me for a moment while I go take a few deep cleansing breaths and type the word GULP in the largest font possible.

I didn't have very long to hyperventilate, however, as, almost immediately after we received permission to begin family-based care, we learned of a little boy I'll call Brandon. At just 2 years of age, he had already lived through more sorrow than any child should have to experience. His father died when he was just a baby, leaving him and his mother without shelter and with little food. They both became weak and malnourished, and sadly his mother passed away from illness just after Brandon's second birthday. Before she died, her last plea was for someone to take care of her baby boy.

LWB immediately stepped in to provide a loving foster home to Brandon, with a local family whose daughters were teens and who was ready and willing to provide care for this little boy.

As Brandon deeply grieved the loss of his mama, his doting foster granny opened her arms and her heart to help him heal. Over time, we saw the light slowly start to return to Brandon's eyes. Within six months of coming into our care, Brandon's smiles and laughter filled his foster home. With good nutrition and medical care, there was now no stopping this continually active little boy.

It was the strong bond he formed with his foster grandma that finally brought true peace and security back to his heart. Except for school time, these two are pretty much inseparable. Brandon loves to sleep in his hammock when he naps, but he always wants his granny to rock him and sing to him as he falls asleep. The two of them also have a small garden that they tend together, although Brandon enjoys eating the food from the garden a little bit more than working in it.

Brandon's case highlights another major difference between running foster care in China versus many other countries around the world. In China, as I've mentioned, most children who end up in orphanage care are abandoned in secret, with little effort being made by local officials to do full and complete birth parent searches. A small "finding ad" is placed in the newspaper and online, but finding ads almost never bring birth parents forward, due to the fears of legal repercussions. It is still the case in 2021 that most children who enter orphanage care in China become long-term wards of the state. New technologies, such as collecting DNA from abandoned children or using facial recognition software to scan abandonment footage captured on street cameras, are starting to lead to a slow increase in identifying possible relatives, but birth parent reunification is still rare.

It is a completely different situation in other regions of the world, however. In a small country like Cambodia, with good detective skills, relatives of abandoned children can often be found. What we've discovered when we have managed to locate a birth parent, however, is that many don't want their children back.

When a divorced or widowed parent remarries in Cambodia, for example, it is quite common for the new spouse to refuse to accept children from a prior marriage. We have seen repeated cases where a mother has chosen her new spouse over even her infant or toddler, resulting in the child being abandoned. These are such complex cases for a charity believing so strongly in the importance of family. Of course, we want reunification with a birth family whenever possible, but what should be done if a child is at risk of re-abandonment if they are returned to a parent who doesn't really want them? With the government having so few social workers on staff, it often falls to us to decide when it's safe to return a child whose birth parent has been found.

This same challenge applies to extended families as well, which is always our second hope for children if the parents are unwilling or unable to care for their child. In Brandon's case, for example, his parents had both died, making him legally an orphan. After searching for extended family, however, we identified an older adult sibling and were hopeful that Brandon could be reunited with a relative who would want to provide him with stability. Very quickly, however, we learned that the sibling only wanted Brandon to use him to beg on the streets. Further investigation showed a pattern of high-risk behaviors. Because every child's case is so completely unique, there are continual discussions with social affairs, law enforcement, and among ourselves as to how to ensure that each child in foster care is best cared for, while working toward reunification **when safe**.

These are rarely black and white issues in Cambodia, especially in the region where LWB is working. Domestic abuse, alcoholism, and drug use are rampant, due to extreme poverty. What constitutes enough neglect or harm to have authorities actually get involved?

In the summer of 2017, I was getting ready to depart Cambodia and was standing with our team near the immigration checkpoint at the border. I saw Leng tense as he looked across the street, and my eyes then fell on an angry man who was dragging a naked little boy violently by his skinny arm. He screamed at the small child and then struck him across his head, before shoving the little boy roughly and yelling some more. It was absolutely horrible to see, and I asked Leng what we could do to stop it.

Leng just shook his head and told me that everyone in that part of town knew this man. He used his small children for begging every day, and, if enough money wasn't raised, he would take all his anger out on the terrified kids. The money the little boys did manage to collect would be used by the dad to buy "ice," a cheap form of meth which is abused heavily in Poipet. Leng told me that it broke his heart that there was nothing he could do to help the boys, as the laws did not allow children to be taken from their parents. We all felt completely helpless as the little boy was dragged down the street.

Over the next few months, Leng would give us updates on the boys whenever he saw them out begging. As the father's addiction worsened, so did his rage, until one day he severely injured the older son. Leng was finally able to convince the local police to get involved, and I can't describe the relief I felt when he messaged that both boys could be placed into our foster care. When Leng went to the police station to pick them up, they were dirty, bruised, and beyond starving. It was then that we learned that they were only 5 and 6 years old. When our medic did his first exam, it became even more clear just how much abuse they had endured.

Hank and Leo quickly embraced living in foster care. They were enrolled in our school, and they soon began making friends in the village. We were amazed at how much they could both eat, and it was wonderful to see their once gaunt faces start to fill out in health.

The boys had been in foster care for just over four months when Leng received a phone call from the authorities. The father had shown up at the police station, promising that he was a changed man and assuring the officers that he would never again hit his sons. It was then that we learned just how quickly a child can be placed back with an abusive parent, as the very next day we were required to turn the boys back over to their dad. They did not want to go, but we sadly learned there was absolutely nothing we could do to postpone the inevitable.

Over the next year, each time we asked about the boys, Leng's voice would get more emotional when he told us they were being used to beg once again. I knew it was incredibly difficult for him to see Hank and Leo suffering in this way, after knowing they had once experienced safety and played with laughter on our school playground before heading home to their caring foster mom. Now they were back to being pulled through the streets by their father, often completely unclothed and crying. We all felt helpless once again.

In the summer of 2019, Leng received a call from authorities that the father was once more abusing drugs. It was only then that we learned that Hank and Leo had two younger siblings; one just a tiny baby whose mother had recently passed away. The police had become involved after learning from concerned neighbors that the children were going without food. The baby girl was severely malnourished and covered with open sores. We would soon learn that she had been infected with HIV, and her father had not bothered to get her started on the essential medication needed to keep the virus in check.

Because the three youngest children were under the age of 6, none of the shelters in the area would accept them, especially since baby Lisa would need close medical monitoring. I'm sure you can guess that Leng said "yes" to moving them into LWB foster care in two seconds flat. When he spoke with us that night, however, he had to break the awful news that the father had decided to keep Hank with him. He agreed to let us take the younger three children but said he needed Hank in order to keep begging for money. We were crushed to discover that, under current Cambodian laws, there was nothing we could do to sever his parental ties, even with known, severe neglect. For now, only Leo and his little siblings have found refuge in our care, but we will never give up hoping that someday Hank will join his siblings and finally have the chance to grow up without fear. We will never quit trying to bring them all together again.

The LWB volunteers who sign up to work in foster care will tell you that this program takes a heavy emotional toll. There are incredible moments of joy, when you see a child like Brandon who has experienced so much loss in his life begin to thrive with stability, access to education, and a devoted foster granny. There is a deep sense of peace in knowing that the newborns we have taken into our care have never experienced the neglect that can come from life in an orphanage…only the support and care of a devoted mom and dad. But there is so much sorrow as well, learning each child's story and trying to process just how many children around the world are truly suffering. Every time LWB is given legal guardianship of a child, we recognize fully just what an enormous responsibility it is to help them begin to heal.

Our team members frequently contact me, saying their deep concern to make the best decision possible for each child keeps them awake at night, to which I know any parent reading this can relate. When you make a commitment to protect a little one's life, there is no getting around the worry for their well-being.

Despite a myriad of challenges, I can say without reservation that LWB foster care in Cambodia is both a highly successful and also ESSENTIAL program in this region. We've taken in children from infants to teens, and every one of them has made remarkable progress with their foster families.

When I think of our family-based care programs, I celebrate the deep commitment that LWB places on every child's life. I am grateful we didn't let fear stop us from doing what is right. I've also come to realize that just like with foster care, where we want every child to develop a deep sense of attachment to their family, it's important to build that same sense of belonging in our communities as well. As humans, we need to feel connected to each other. I've seen that uniting for a common purpose can bring people together in remarkable ways. When people feel committed to a cause, the strength of community can really shine through.

In 2016, LWB began helping children in the East African country of Uganda, where over 1.2 million children have lost parents from HIV alone. Similar to Cambodia, a brutal civil war left enormous scars on Uganda's society and infrastructure, from its education system to healthcare. Its medical system deteriorated in the 1970s and 80s, and, in rural regions still today, there is only one doctor for every 22,000 people (compared to one for every 39 people in the US). Slow access to health services for children can often have devastating consequences, with pneumonia, malaria, and diarrhea contributing to a still-too-high mortality rate for children under age 5.

One of the first children referred to us for medical care in Uganda was a girl named Grace. She lived in an extremely remote village near the border of Rwanda, accessible only by boat. When I first received her picture, I immediately was drawn to her beautiful but extremely solemn face. I then gave a little gasp when I saw that her abdomen was so swollen that it looked like it would rupture at any moment. She was a thin 14-year-old, wearing a small yellow sweatshirt, but her exposed abdomen looked like she was carrying sextuplets, with every vein visible and bulging.

While we will never know exactly what happened, we believe Grace had a teratoma, a type of tumor which is often benign at first. Grace's mother was unable to get her care locally, finally traveling with Grace many hours away to find a doctor willing to take her case. An immediate operation to remove the tumor from near her ovary was planned. During the surgery, it is possible that the abnormal growth ruptured, "seeding" her abdomen with thousands of small tumor cells.

Over the next several years, her abdomen grew more distended, reaching the point where it was difficult to sit or even breathe. The pain she felt from her swelling abdomen eventually caused her to drop out of school, an enormous loss for Grace as she is so intelligent and curious about life.

Three separate times, a doctor tried to drain the fluid from her abdomen, but unfortunately that only treated the symptoms, and the tumors continued to multiply. Grace needed very specialized surgery which couldn't occur in her home country, and here is where the LWB community stepped forward yet again.

Thanks to one of our board members who was a physician, we were able to connect with a charity hospital in Kenya, who then introduced us to a doctor at MD Anderson Cancer Center in Texas. Dr. Andrea Hayes-Jordan is not only the first African American female pediatric surgeon in the United States, she is also one of the world's leading experts on desmoplastic small round cell tumors (DSRCT), a rare cancer which spreads throughout a child's abdominal and chest cavity. She pioneered efforts to create new surgery protocols to help children with this condition who were once deemed inoperable.

Originally, I thought we were consulting with Dr. Hayes-Jordan for advice on Grace's medical needs, but then we got the amazing news that she was willing to fly all the way to Kenya to do Grace's surgery herself. We were overjoyed that Grace would have this special opportunity at being healed. Dr. Hayes-Jordan told us that Grace would need an eight- to twelve-hour operation to strip all the tiny tumors from the lining of her abdomen, and then she would circulate a continuous infusion of heated chemotherapy drugs throughout Grace's abdominal cavity to kill any cells that might be left behind. Because no hospital in East Africa had the specialized equipment needed, she planned to use the Kenya hospital's heart bypass machine to do the chemo wash for Grace instead.

We immediately reached out to our supporters, letting them know about Grace and the rare opportunity that was unfolding for her to receive the operation she needed. With exceptional generosity, they funded her entire surgery cost. As I watched so many kind donations being made, I kept thinking about the thousands of children we had helped through the years who had also needed someone to believe in them. Seeing their transformations in China encouraged LWB to expand to new locations, leading us to Grace. To think that a girl from a rural village in Uganda was going to be helped by a surgeon from America flying all the way to a hospital in Kenya…well, that was the very definition of "love without boundaries" to me.

Grace's journey to Kenya, of course, was not a simple one. By the time we first met her, she was extremely weak and fatigued. The thousands of small tumors in her abdomen were sapping her energy and strength, and she was suffering from malnutrition. She needed to be in the best health possible before undergoing a ten plus hour operation, and so we helped move Grace and her mom from their small mud home across the lake to a temporary apartment next door to one of our local team members. For the next month, Grace received lots of fruits, vegetables, and protein, and thankfully she quickly began gaining new vigor.

The next big issue was getting permission for Grace to leave Uganda for the surgery. Because she was born in an extremely remote village, Grace did not have a formal birth certificate. Thus began a series of visits to the appropriate offices to first get a formal certificate of birth and then to get all the IDs and travel passes needed for Grace and her mom to cross the border into Kenya. Once that was completed, airline reservations were made, and it seemed like everything was coming together perfectly. In July 2017, they traveled by car across the entire length of Uganda to reach the airport city of Entebbe, where a few more hurdles then arose.

Grace and her mom discovered they needed yellow fever vaccination certificates to cross the border into Kenya. Thankfully, a visit to a nearby clinic solved that issue quickly. At the airport, however, an airline employee took one look at Grace's enormous abdomen and said she couldn't board the flight without a formal letter stating she had medical clearance to leave the country. Thank goodness for the power of the Internet! Within a few short hours, we had letters from physicians in the US and Kenya explaining how urgent her case was. Early the next morning Grace, her mom, and our team member Shallon flew on an airplane for the first time in their lives. After landing in Nairobi, they then traveled many more hours by car until finally reaching Tenwek Hospital in Bomet. The medical team soon gathered to finalize the surgery plan.

Grace's complex operation took an unthinkable 24 hours. Dr. Hayes-Jordan told us that Grace's abdomen was filled with literally thousands of tiny tumors, all making a mucus type fluid and "sticking" to the lining that covers the abdominal organs. She needed to carefully strip the peritoneum by hand to remove the tumor cells while leaving the organs intact.

Although it was mentally and physically exhausting to stand in the OR for that length of time, Dr. Hayes-Jordan felt that she had removed all the tumors she could find. Her only concern was that the temperature of the chemotherapy drugs which were circulated throughout Grace's abdomen did not reach the ideal 105 to 107 degrees because of a lack of adequate equipment at the hospital. Grace's "wash" had been done at just 102 degrees, but everyone remained hopeful that the surgery would prove successful.

Immediately after the operation, Grace seemed to recover surprisingly well. She received lots of fluids to help clear the chemotherapy drugs from her system. She woke up and responded to her mom by nodding her head to simple questions. Then, within a few short hours, her kidneys began to struggle and she had to be intubated again. At first, the doctors felt this was normal because of the massive amounts of chemo drugs going through her kidneys, but by the next day the doctors became much more concerned as Grace's body began to fill with fluid. Even her hands swelled to the point of not being able to bend her fingers. Infection soon set in as well, and we asked the entire LWB community to pray.

A few days later, we received very hopeful news from our team member Shallon. She wrote:

Three miracles happened this evening.

First, Grace was helped to sit up on the bed and supported herself with her hands on both sides.

Second, she asked with sign language for a pen and a piece of paper. We gave them to her, and she began to write. She was distracted by trying to focus on the paper while coughing from the irritating tubes that are deep in her abdomen through the mouth. From my observation, I felt she was trying to write my name. We asked if she really was, and she nodded her head with a sign of yes.

The third miracle was her request for food. She used sign language to tell us that she wanted to eat food. Not water, but food. We told her that we thought the doctors would allow her to have food tomorrow. We told her to stand strong only for tonight if she could.

She requested for me to hold her like giving her a hug. I did it, and she kept on holding my hands to hold her tightly on each side. Then I touched my head to her forehead and prayed with her.

Her mum held her for a long time with a hug after me.

For the next few weeks, I know people around the world waited with bated breath for news that Grace had truly turned the corner. We cheered each small sign of improvement…from her first bites of potatoes to taking a few steps from her hospital bed. The photos sent to me from Kenya showed Grace's steady progress, until I finally received one that let us all exhale. Grace was standing tall, with a now completely flat stomach, holding a pink flamingo toy gifted by a caring nurse. She radiated joy with a beautiful smile which lit up her entire face.

After facing multiple post-op complications from everything her body had endured, Grace and her mom were finally able to leave the hospital two months after arriving in Kenya. She returned home to Uganda a completely different girl, full of energy and life, and counting down the days until she could once again enroll in school.

In the fall of 2017, LWB arranged for Grace to attend a top primary school in her region. When she first walked into a classroom again after being out for several years, she understandably earned low marks that were well behind those of her peers. Grace had decided on her future dream, however, when she was in the hospital recovering. She set a goal to become a doctor herself someday, to help others just like her. Grace worked nonstop at her studies, determined to prove her ability to both her teachers and her classmates.

At the end of her second year back in school, we received Grace's new report card. We sat in awe looking at the paper which showed Grace had earned the number one position in her grade out of 68 students in her class. Isn't that incredible? Grace was relentless in her goal of becoming a well-educated woman, and we couldn't wait to see everything she was going to accomplish.

At the beginning of 2019, however, Grace's abdomen began to swell again. She was understandably devastated by the symptoms she was once again feeling in her body, and, as her stomach grew bigger, she became even more despondent. It seemed her abdomen was enlarging with each passing day, and her chest began to change shape as well. She started wanting to be alone and even said she was going to drop out of school as the other children noticed the swelling and began taunting her, insisting she was pregnant. We tried to assure her that she just needed to concentrate on her education while we searched for the medical care she might need, but she spent most of her days in tears.

As quickly as possible, we arranged for Grace to be seen by Dr. Martin Situma, a remarkable pediatric surgeon in Uganda. It is hard to believe, but with a population of 22 million children, there are just six pediatric surgeons in the entire country. They are understandably in huge demand.

Dr. Situma arranged for a CT scan of Grace's abdomen, and we soon received the news we had been dreading. Grace's tumors had indeed returned, and they were multiplying rapidly.

We reached out to experts far and wide for opinions on whether a second operation for Grace would even be possible. Her kidneys had struggled so much to recover following her first surgery in Kenya. Could her body undergo another difficult round of tumor removal and chemotherapy?

As we investigated every possibility, we found our way to Dr. Wim Ceelen, a senior surgical oncologist at Ghent University in Belgium. We soon discovered that he is one of the best in the world at performing HIPEC (Hyperthermic Intraperitoneal Chemotherapy), the same abdominal wash procedure Grace had undergone in Kenya. He was willing to review Grace's medical files but also told us upfront that he would not put her through such a major operation if he felt she wasn't a good candidate for the repeat procedure.

He reached out to Dr. Hayes-Johnson about the first surgery that had been done, while we gathered more medical files and test results. We then waited on pins and needles for his answer. After a very thorough review, he accepted Grace for surgery in Belgium. This was an absolute answer to prayer, but I also knew that such a complicated procedure in Europe would come at a much higher cost than the one performed at a mission hospital in Kenya. I exchanged multiple emails with the hospital finance office in Ghent, with everyone trying to get the price of the surgery within the realm of possibility for a children's charity. Would we be able to raise the funds for Grace to go through the same complex procedure once more?

The title of this chapter is *Commitment*, and our wonderful supporters proved yet again that they believe the lives of vulnerable children are important. Grace was part of the LWB family, and we couldn't let her down. As soon as we announced that her only opportunity at healing meant getting her to Belgium, our supporters responded loud and clear that Grace was absolutely worthy of this second chance. When our community's passion for helping children is combined with a true commitment to seeing things through, I've seen firsthand that anything is possible.

In the spring of 2019, we finalized the agreement with Ghent University and wired all the needed funds for Grace to receive surgery. Of course, just like the first time, there were a few more logistics to work out, such as getting Grace a passport. She had to make several long trips to Uganda's capital for the paperwork, but thankfully everything was approved with only a few small hiccups. We then had to ask Belgium to grant Grace a medical visa, not always easy from

Uganda, but the staff at the consulate in Kampala worked nonstop to expedite everything.

The biggest worry we had, however, was sending Grace and her mom to Europe, since they had never left east Africa and didn't speak English. Would they be able to make the flight connections and find their way to the hospital? In a remarkable series of events (oh, how I love the Internet), we connected with a kind man named Mark who lived in Belgium. He was not only from Uganda but from the exact same region as Grace and her mom. This meant that he spoke the same rare Rakiga dialect as Grace, which only 5% of Ugandans do! He agreed to pick them up at the airport when they arrived and get them safely to the hospital. It gave me goosebumps to see everything come together for Grace to get this opportunity.

At 1 am on April 2nd, after 18 long hours in the OR, Grace's surgery to remove the extensive abdominal tumors was completed in Belgium. Her mom was able to be right by her bedside in the ICU and was so relieved that Grace had come through such a long and complex second operation.

Dr. Ceelen reported that he painstakingly removed all visible tumors within Grace's abdomen and then performed the chemotherapy circulation, in the hopes that any remaining non-visible tumors would be eradicated. This time, the equipment used was able to keep the chemo drugs at the ideal hot temperature needed to optimally target all remaining tumor cells.

The very next morning, Grace was able to get the breathing tube out of her throat, and even sip some apple juice. She gave Dr. Ceelen a big smile and was able to talk to him when he came by to see her. He told us he was awed by her courage and strength. Grace told him that she had a dream about singing in church while she was sleeping, and we took that as a sign that she would be standing and singing again soon.

Two years after her surgery in Belgium, Grace remains tumor free. Every time she sends a message to our team, she asks us to express her gratitude to everyone who made her life-changing operation possible. While COVID has caused most schools in Uganda to suspend classes, Grace remains diligent in her studies at home. Once her school is given permission to reopen, we will be right there to make sure she can continue her dream of someday graduating from high school and being the first in her family to attend university.

Isn't that the beauty of commitment? It keeps us focused on what we value and ties us to something bigger than our individual selves. While each of us must decide on our own which causes or communities deserve our dedication, when we commit ourselves to doing whatever we can to make this world a better place, our lives fill with purpose and a powerful feeling of hope.

Chapter 4: Innovation

"Innovation is always learning and trying to get better every day. Challenge the status quo and how things have always been done, even in your own life, and be courageous to change things for the better."

Charlie Guo, LWB Board member

In the fall of 2015, a young woman working as a migrant worker in southeast China went into labor. She and her husband, both just 20 years old, were members of the Yi ethnic minority from far western China. They had traveled almost 600 miles from their impoverished rural village to search for work to support themselves and their parents back home. The exhausted mom was scared. The pain from her abdomen had intensified as they made their way by bus to the nearest hospital.

Later that evening, the couple's lives changed forever when twin baby boys were delivered into the world. The struggling couple had not been able to afford an ultrasound during pregnancy and were overjoyed by the surprise arrival of this double blessing. Very quickly, however, the mood of the medical team in the delivery room changed. It was discovered that the tiny boys had been born conjoined, an extremely rare condition which occurs when a fertilized egg only partially splits into identical twins. In the case of newly arrived Harley and James, their bodies remained fused together at the pelvis.

In many hospitals in China, medical treatment will not be given until the funds for a procedure are paid up front. Understandably, Harley and James' parents had no savings for the twins' unexpected medical needs. The father begged his family and friends back home for help, borrowing money from everyone he knew in their rural farming village to pay for his new sons' mounting expenses. Soon, however, the twins' bill grew so high that the hospital knew the poverty-stricken couple would not be able to cover the costs.

The very next day, the little boys were discharged from the maternity hospital. The young parents, too afraid to return yet to their village, then made their way to Shanghai with the boys, after hearing that surgeons there had successfully separated other conjoined twins. Of course, when informed by the hospital what the cost of such a complicated procedure would be, they felt completely hopeless.

It was then that they met our Shanghai medical manager, Li Ping, who told them that LWB would be honored to try to help their sons receive their separation surgery. He encouraged them to return home to their village in Guizhou for the upcoming spring festival and assured them that throughout the holiday we would work hard to raise the needed funds.

We didn't realize when they left Shanghai for their rural home that it would be a three-day walk from the closest train station to their village. To save money, they found a small house that was scheduled to be demolished. The building had no electricity or heat, and the parents worked hard to keep the twins warm and healthy as best they could.

The photos they sent us of their living situation alarmed us greatly, as they were sleeping together on the hard floor with the babies. When we learned that they were looking for scraps of wood and leaves to burn for heat, we quickly sent some money to be sure they could purchase food and firewood. The fundraising for their surgery ramped up immediately.

When we first let our supporters know about Harley and James, we could not have imagined the international outpouring of love and concern for these special twins. Donations started arriving from people all over the world who gave what they could to make sure the boys received their separation surgery. We were especially touched to hear from three 9-year-old girls in Ireland. Sophie, Roisin, and Zoe had learned about the little twins and decided they wanted to make a difference. They and their classmates each knitted one red square, which they then joined together to make a special blanket to auction off for funding. When the winner of the blanket told the girls they could keep their homemade creation and send it to the twins in China, the students immediately got to work on a second blanket as well, so that each boy could have his own. With love like this being shown, is it any wonder that within a few short weeks all the funding needed for the twins' operation was in place?

Getting the boys back to Shanghai proved to be quite a challenge, however, as it was not only winter in their mountainous town, but also Chinese New Year. First, a major snowstorm blocked the single road out of their village, making all travel impossible. Then, once the roads were clear, the family missed the train they were supposed to take back to Shanghai. With all train seats sold out for the month due to the mass migration of people during the lunar new year, there was a brief panic over whether they would make it to the hospital in time for their scheduled pre-op appointments.

Thankfully, we were able to get them on a flight instead, which ended up being quite the adventure as it was the very first time in their lives they had ever traveled by plane. Any parent who knows how difficult it can be to travel with one child on your lap on narrow plane seats can imagine that it was doubly difficult to figure out how to hold the conjoined twins on the long flight. The parents took 20-minute shifts trying to keep the babies comfortable on their laps. We all celebrated when they finally arrived, exhausted but truly hopeful, at the Children's Hospital of Fudan University.

One of our wonderful LWB volunteers in Shanghai, Sherri Cox, soon went to visit the twins and their parents in the hospital. She wrote:

> *The twins are in a private room on an inner corridor. Unfortunately, they are still a novelty, and a steady stream of people keep coming by to see that they are really conjoined and take photos.*
>
> *I was able to show them the twins' donation page on my iPad. They pointed to the dollar signs on the right hand side and looked at me for an explanation. I told them that 817 people, from all over the world, had gone online and donated money. I could tell this news deeply affected them because they swallowed hard and became quiet while the realization sunk in that so many people that they have never met truly care about their little boys.*
>
> *They were also told the story of the little girls in Ireland raising money for Harley and James. We had printed out the photo of all their Irish classmates holding the blanket and talked about the whole school rooting for them. They looked at all of the children's faces, commenting how some looked Indian, some Chinese, and others European. They seemed surprised that kids of different ethnic backgrounds were all together in one classroom, and they also seemed amazed by how broad the web of support for them extends.*
>
> *I asked about their sleeping arrangements and learned they are all sleeping together in the single hospital bed. I should mention how difficult it is to get these babies to sleep. The family works so hard to soothe them, but when you are literally attached to your brother, it is understandably hard.*

A lot of the time, the babies hold hands, but many times they are flailing a hand into the other's face or sticking a finger in the other's eye or mouth. Li Ping and I were trying to 'shush' the constant visitors who were coming in because their voices would wake one child, who would then wake the other. I am sure these babies will sleep so much better when they are no longer conjoined.

As detailed testing and scans got underway, we learned that in addition to sharing one pelvic structure, Harley and James had only one liver. They also had intestines which were partially fused. The imaging scans were not able to give an exact picture of the babies' bladders, but the medical team remained hopeful there were two.

Doctors from the departments of orthopedics, anesthesiology, urology, and general surgery all met together to come up with the best path forward for the boys, as their rare anatomy had never been seen before. It was then that we saw how truly innovative the team at Fudan was. They decided to use new 3-D printing technology to create a life-sized model of the twins' complex anatomy, printed directly from their scans. When I first saw the completed model of the boys' pelvic cavity, I could only say, "Wow!" The details were extraordinary. Using the new technology empowered the medical team to develop a precise surgery plan, which gave new insights into possible complications. As they studied the 3-D model in front of them, however, they knew it would be one of the most difficult operations ever undertaken at the hospital.

On a cold February morning in Shanghai, at 8:10 am, Harley and James were wheeled into the operating room and placed onto a single surgical table. Their parents had given the boys a final goodbye hug and now anxiously waited outside the OR doors, gripping each other's hands and praying their sons would survive the long operation ahead.

Over the next eight hours, orthopedic surgeons worked carefully to separate the pelvic cavity, followed by a team of general surgeons who stepped in to separate the liver and intestines. At 4:20

in the afternoon, the twins officially became two individual babies. Harley was handed off to waiting surgeons and his own OR table, and then each boy's independent operation began.

Urologists painstakingly undertook the difficult task of repairing the twins' unique bladders so that each baby could have their own urinary tract. The boys were then handed off once more to a new team of surgeons, who created temporary colostomies for the boys. Finally, the orthopedic team returned yet again to begin constructing a separate pelvis for each of the twins. The surgery went three hours longer than expected, but late that evening Harley and James were moved into the pediatric ICU.

Before the operation, the medical team had marked each boy's forehead with a different colored dot to help everyone know who was who after separation. It was a bit surreal to glimpse James (with a red dot) and Harley (marked with blue) each in their own individual incubator after only seeing them entwined for the past several months. Both boys remained on ventilators to give them extra assistance with their breathing, but doctors assured us that each was quite stable.

The next morning, their parents were allowed to go into the ICU to see their now separate babies for the very first time. Can you even imagine their relief? They couldn't stop smiling and touching their little boys, and it was a wondrous moment when mom and dad were soon allowed to each hold a baby in their arms.

Every update we received on the twins over the next few years brought joy. Harley and James became two highly active toddlers, adored to the moon and back by their still grateful parents. They told us their sons are nonstop busy, first learning to walk and then energetically run. Their mom said they still have a special bond between them, where they always seem to know what the other is thinking. Even though their parents are still only in their 20s, I have a feeling the mischievous nature of these adorable twin boys will give them more than a few gray hairs. It sure makes me smile. For the rest of my life, whenever I think of Harley and James, I will forever be amazed that the supporters of LWB, coupled with the incredible ingenuity and skills of the doctors in Shanghai, helped make their now unlimited futures a reality.

Of course, we expect researchers and physicians to solve complex problems by using their scientific minds. Thank goodness for university labs, state-of-the-art technology, and all the brilliant research being conducted around the world by those wanting to make a difference. I've seen firsthand through LWB's work in often very remote regions, however, that innovative solutions also arise in everyday communities when local people come together and simply think outside the box.

In fall 2016, I flew into Kigali, Rwanda, as it was the closest airport to the rural village I had been invited to visit in far southwest Uganda.

After a several hours' journey to the border, I found myself on a final dusty road, heading up a mountain to meet approximately 120 rural families in Karu Village. I had been told that many of the children living there were in extremely vulnerable conditions, as at least one of their parents had passed away, many from HIV.

The villagers I would spend the next four days with were from the Bakiga tribe, known as the "people of the mountains." They call themselves the toughest, hardest working people in Uganda due to the many challenges in their lives. They must run down cliffs to fetch water; dig through hard, rocky soil to grow crops on terraced hillsides; and gather wood which they carry on their heads to use as fuel. As we pulled up to the top of the hill, over a hundred children were waiting to greet us. I will never forget the joyous singing which met us as we stepped out of the truck.

During that week, as we discussed with the local villagers how LWB might assist the children, one word was mentioned repeatedly as being an essential need. One word, with five simple letters, that many of us so often take for granted.

So… have you had a drink of water yet today? Or how about a shower? Did you even give it a second thought as you turned on the tap and watched the H2O pour out? I will admit with great remorse that, before my first trip to Africa, I hardly gave water a second thought.

If you take nothing else away from this book, I hope you will occasionally give a prayer of thanks for the abundance of available water with which most of us in the West are blessed. From the moment I first crossed the dusty border into Uganda, there was one constant sight no matter where I looked: yellow plastic jugs, called jerry cans. Almost everyone walking on the side of the road had one in their hands or up on their heads. Bicycles going by had six to eight strapped to their sides. You don't go anywhere without one, as they hold the precious substance our bodies need the most.

You probably already know that we can live more than three weeks without taking in any food but less than a week without water to drink. For the children in the remote village I was visiting, access to water was one of their greatest difficulties.

Our host that week in the village was a young man named Innocent. He had been born with a club foot, which was seen as a sign of being cursed. In order to keep bad luck from entering the village, the local witch doctor had taken the newborn out into the bushes and left him to his fate. Thankfully, an elderly grandma passing by heard the now howling baby, and Innocent's life was saved. As he grew up, he knew he wanted to help change things in his village, bringing education and new ways of thinking to the next generation.

Innocent shared with us that the children in Karu village still had to walk a very long way, down a dangerous mountain path, to fetch the water their families needed. For the younger children and women who were elderly or heavily pregnant, it could take up to four hours of their day. EVERY single day.

I had traveled with one of our directors from China, Cindy Wu, and we asked Innocent if we could possibly do the water run with the children after school one day. He told us he felt it would be too difficult and even risky for us since the path could be quite treacherous. We felt we really needed to join the children, though, to better understand this pressing need, and so he agreed to take us the next day.

I had no idea what to expect, but I smile now thinking of the local men gathering at the top of the hill the next afternoon, taking bets on whether or not the two foreigners would make it down to the valley and then back up the mountain. Cindy had grown up in a rural village in southern China when she was a little girl, back when communal wells were common, so she jokingly flexed her muscles and told me that country East would certainly beat city West.

I was saying a little prayer that I wouldn't let my country down as the children in the village ran to get their five-gallon jerry cans. Many of the children planned to carry two. Just to give you some reference, a single gallon of water weighs about 8.3 pounds, so once those plastic jugs were filled, the older children would be carrying over 80 pounds each up the mountain.

I looked around to see which yellow can I could carry, insisting over their protests that I had to contribute and bring needed water back up the hill. I tried not to take it personally when they ran over with a "baby water can" to carry, because they were so confident that I would never make it back up with a normal sized one. It looked like a child's toy, and the villagers were all laughing as I picked it up with a shrug of my shoulders. We were told from the moment a child learns to walk, they also learn to carry water. For as my new friends told me once again, *"Without water... there can be no life."*

We left the village at 5:05 pm that day, which gave us just under three hours until it would be dark. As we walked down the rocky trail, I tried to pay close attention to where the children in front of me stepped so I could try and copy their path to keep from slipping. I was trying to wrap my mind around the children doing this walk every single day for two hours in the morning and two hours at night. I was even more saddened to learn that many children begin the walk in complete darkness, relying on the light of the moon in order to not fall on the path.

Since most village homes don't have a clock, children rely on the sound of roosters to wake up. If a rooster mistakenly crows at 3 am, the children hop up on autopilot and start down the trail, not knowing the real time. I was told it is not uncommon to find children sleeping down at the water source due to getting there before the sunrise.

Many stories were told to me about children who had been injured falling down the hills. In fact, the village has a special drumbeat they sound whenever someone is injured fetching water, calling all villagers to come and help. If someone has broken a leg, for example, they will have to carry the person on a twig stretcher over their heads up the mountain.

Several children came up to show me the scars on their bodies they had received from falling and being injured while making the trek. During the rainy season, the danger increases exponentially as the dusty dirt path turns to a wet and slippery mud. Innocent pointed out a little girl heading down the path in front of us named Gabby, wearing a frayed green sweater and hurrying down the rocky trail in her bare feet. Her family lives in one of the steepest areas of the village, making the daily trek for water particularly difficult. Tragically, Gabby's father died falling off the side of a cliff one evening as he was bringing water home in the dark.

In addition to the physical toll the lack of access to water has on the villagers, there are other deep implications as well. The great amount of time women and children spend fetching water keeps them from both school and income-producing activities. It also often limits the number of meals a child receives to just one per day. For many children, they wake up before 5 am to do the water run, returning home with their plastic jerry can for the family and then running in the opposite direction for school. There is no time for breakfast, so they start their school day extremely hungry, often having nothing since lunch the day before.

There are often fights at the water area as well, as older children push the younger ones out of the way so they can run back home and make it to school on time. If you are late to the public school far from the village, you can be punished severely, so having to wait in line to fill your water jug can be very stressful indeed.

The United Nations has set ten gallons of water per person per day as the minimum amount needed for health and survival. For this particular village, five gallons a day per person was the goal. For little children who are carrying 1.2-gallon jugs (like I was), they must make four trips up and down the mountain to reach that five-gallon target. I later learned that the average American uses **100 gallons of water per person,** every single day.

It took us just under an hour to walk down the mountain to the valley water source and then another 20 minutes to fill up our plastic cans. We were quickly running out of time to get back before dark, so the kids swiftly motioned for me to grab my baby water can (now filled to ten pounds), and we began the trek.

We climbed straight up the mountain for over 30 minutes, and I will admit that I was panting pretty hard at that point, not only from the physical stress but also because, just like the villagers, I hadn't had water to drink yet that afternoon. The children must have heard my breathing, as, when the path widened a bit on the side of a rocky cliff, they grabbed onto my hand and motioned for me to take a rest. I was more than happy to put down my now surprisingly heavy jug, while feeling guilty that I was slowing them all down. We sat on the side of the mountain, overlooking a steep drop-off. No matter which direction I looked, there were people going up and down the mountain paths to get water.

While we sat and looked at the view, I decided to play some music on my phone, and the teen girls sitting next to me giggled and seemed to like the pop band One Direction just as much as my youngest daughter did back in Florida. I love how music can bring us all together even without a common language.

The next song that came up on my phone was "Moves Like Jagger" by Maroon 5, and there was something about the beat which caused 7-year-old Julian to suddenly jump up and start dancing. I had been worried about this little boy since the moment I first met him, as he was painfully thin and had crusty sores on his head. Despite his frail appearance, Julian was a master dancer. We all shared a wonderful laugh watching him move and shake to the completely new rhythm.

Our rest stop on the mountain was costing precious time as the sun began to go down, so once more we grabbed our water jugs and began climbing. Two hours and 45 minutes after we first started down the path, we emerged back on top. I consider myself in my 50s to be in fairly decent shape, since I try to exercise every day, but this was a climb like I'd never done before. As excited as I was to have made it back up to the village, I quickly faced the reality that we had only gotten enough water to last until morning – when the children would once again have to head down the hillside.

If you are like me, you are probably already thinking to yourself, "This village should have a well." That was, of course, the first solution that quickly came to my mind, but the leaders in the village then explained that, despite repeated attempts over the years, they had never had success in getting a well to produce water. I soon learned the sobering truth that NGOs have spent billions of dollars digging wells in Africa, but the reality is that far too many fall into disrepair in a short period of time. Some researchers have reported that over half of the wells that have been dug in Africa are in non-working order, due to broken parts, corrosion, and sinking water pipes. It usually isn't as simple as coming in to dig a well and then bidding the project goodbye.

There had to be a solution, however. I remembered words I had once heard that, *"No company has ever created an innovation; it's people who do."* So, we brainstormed with the villagers and our community on how to bring a sustainable solution to the children of Karu Village. The ideas started flowing, and I saw again that innovation happens when people aren't afraid to take a completely different path. We had all been so fixated on figuring out a solution to build a working well that we overlooked the fact that every family was already storing water in five-gallon yellow jugs. We quickly switched to investigating water storage methods instead and began formulating a plan with Innocent on how to collect the precious drops of rain that regularly fell from the sky.

Rainwater harvesting, of course, has been around for centuries, but it had never been done with families in the village, as most lived in simple, mud huts with grass roofs. To successfully harvest rain, you need a hard roofing material which the water can run across, collecting into gutters before funneling into a large barrel. We began researching everything we could find on the best systems for this region and soon set our sights on purchasing a 100-gallon storage tank for every family on the mountain.

While we were raising funds for the project, the people in the village were adding sheets of metal to their roofs and coming up with ways to connect PVC piping to make sure every home was included. Neighbors helped neighbors, knowing that having ready access to water would have a huge impact on their community. Thanks to the generosity of our supporters, by the fall of 2017, the rainwater harvesting system was fully in place. The children in the village were ecstatic.

When a rainwater tank was delivered to little Daniel's family, he jumped around cheering. "Even if I don't have to go down to the river for a whole week, that's enough," he said. "It will be a real holiday for us!" Six-year-old Doris' mother told us that all of her children have had to work extremely hard to fetch water, not only for their own family but for their elderly grandma as well. As she looked at her newly installed water collection unit, she felt fresh hope for her daughter. "This one is not going to spend her life fetching water," she said proudly. "This one is going to study."

Access to water is such a basic human right, and the rainwater project forever changed the way I look at our most essential resource. I'll find myself sometimes looking at the multiple sinks in my home with a sense of shame, remembering the children in Karu Village walking up and down hillsides with their yellow jerry cans, in search of this life-giving fluid. I will never forget how, despite all their hardships, they welcomed us with songs that echoed down the mountain. When I think of their beautiful faces, I give thanks that through the creative minds of both the villagers and our international community, an effective solution to a decades-old problem was found.

After having been in the charity world for almost 20 years, I can say with certainty that it is not a world that praises failure. It is rare to see a charity actually come out and say, "Well, that certainly didn't work," understandably worried that funders will not return.

I like to think that mistakes are often the absolute best learning moments, however. When a project doesn't go exactly as planned, it can then lead us to discover even greater solutions. I remind myself that Thomas Edison once said, *"I have not failed. I've just found 10,000 ways that won't work."* Thankfully for our Sokhem Village school in Cambodia, we didn't need 10,000 tries to fix a major problem we first encountered. Instead, we learned yet again that sometimes our missteps can have real silver linings. As long as you never give up trying to change an injustice, new and even visionary solutions can be found.

As I wrote earlier, LWB built our first Believe in Me school in Cambodia directly in the heart of rural Sokhem Village. Each day, as the children would gather to watch the construction, we would receive photos of the older girls excitedly showing the little brothers and sisters carried on their hips that school would be opening soon. As they came to enroll, they again brought their baby siblings, marking an "X" on the papers for their signature, while effortlessly shifting the infants and toddlers onto their backs. We definitely should have taken more notice versus just commenting on the cuteness of all the babies, as, on the very first day of classes, almost half the older children in the village proudly arrived at school and took their seats with a younger sibling planted firmly in their laps. Yep… that was a wee bit of a problem we hadn't fully considered. Their parents left the village each day to search for work in Thailand, so I don't know where we had expected all the babies to go during class time. It was more than a little misstep, but we quickly began asking the question of what solutions could be found.

I sincerely believe that at LWB we've built a charity where everyone feels safe to throw out and exchange ideas. No one is ever discouraged from offering new suggestions on how to improve our programs for the kids. We regularly ask for help in our community, as I feel so strongly that listening to the ideas of others is what empowers innovation. The author Brené Brown once wisely wrote on the importance of deeply listening: *"Do you want to be right or do you want to get it right?"*

I wrote to all the volunteers with LWB at that time and told them about the current situation we had in Sokhem and how we didn't feel the older children could fully embrace their education while they were having to babysit at school. Almost immediately, I received a reply saying, "It's a shame we can't have a little school for the younger siblings built right next door, so the older kids could focus on their lessons without interruptions." Oh, yes, ingenuity at its finest. While it had never been done in this region of Cambodia, we worked with our local team on the ground to design a quality daycare program for infants and toddlers, so their older brothers and sisters could concentrate on their studies.

In addition to providing a safe place for the babies to be cared for during the day, our new "Sibling School" would provide high-quality formula and meals to further combat chronic malnutrition. By hiring local women to serve as caregivers in the new daycare, some of the mothers would be able to stay in the village each day, rather than taking the risk to cross into Thailand, often illegally, where they face exploitation and abuse. It was an innovative solution that would go on to impact the entire community…from infants, to school-aged children, to their parents.

    As this program has grown, the original Sibling School transformed into the Sokhem Village Early Childhood Development Center, with over 60 infants and toddlers now enrolled. Through the initial mistake of not fully anticipating the caregiver roles of the local children, we have now created a comprehensive childhood program in the village to help newborns to teens. The results are indisputable. When we first became involved with this rural location back in 2016, the childhood malnutrition rate was at 75%. We have reduced that number to zero. The results are the same for mortality rates in kids under age 5, which significantly decreased as well. There have been no childhood deaths in the village since LWB became involved.

    Our Sokhem Village program can now provide services to vulnerable children in the surrounding areas as well, and one of the first families who comes to mind is 10-year-old Jana's. Our team had originally met her living in a makeshift settlement which had sprung up during COVID on public lands. Dozens of families, left in abject poverty due to the pandemic, had built temporary shelters made of tarps and sheets of metal. We soon learned that Jana, her siblings, and her mother had fled their home several hours away to escape domestic violence. With no real plan on how they would survive, Jana's mom had found a dilapidated structure for the family to sleep in. Soon after arriving at the settlement, she left her children at the border to go searching for work.

    On the day we came upon the children, Jana had been left in charge of her three little brothers for almost a week. She told our team that their meager food supplies were now gone, so she had been taking water from the dirty creek to feed her baby brother Micah. She hoped the water would fill his stomach enough to make his cries of hunger stop.

    Jana and her little brothers showed clear signs of chronic malnutrition. Jana's hair was thinning and discolored, and the baby's abdomen was distended. Our medic confirmed that the children needed urgent nutritional intervention, as little Micah weighed just 11 pounds at 8 months of age.

Our team returned repeatedly to the border region over the next few weeks to make sure this vulnerable family had the food supplies they needed. On one of the visits, Jana shyly shared that she'd never been to school since she had to take care of her brothers while her mom searched for day labor. She dreamed of someday learning to read, and we of course wanted to help her make that wish a reality.

We knew our education campus in Sokhem Village would be the perfect fit for the four children, as Jana and her two older brothers could attend the primary school while baby Micah was safely cared for at the early childhood center. There was one major obstacle to that plan, however: the family's makeshift home was far from Sokhem Village. We knew we couldn't let that challenge get in the way of their health or Jana's dream.

Hooray for our LWB tuk-tuks, motorcycle school buses, which can head out to the most remote villages. One of our wonderful tuk-tuk drivers agreed to make the journey to the border settlement each day to pick up Jana and her brothers, finally letting them have the chance to go to school.

Now, every morning before the sun rises, Jana and her siblings wake up and proudly put on their school uniforms. They are safely driven into Sokhem Village, where they spend their entire day at our schools and have access to a healthy breakfast and lunch. Their once discolored hair is now a vibrant shade of black, and baby Micah has gained significant weight and energy, with his nannies cheering him on as he drains every bottle.

We could end this story of hope right here... just knowing that Jana and her little brothers are now receiving not only education but good nutrition as well. But it gets even better than that, which happens so often when the LWB community opens its welcoming arms even wider.

You see, Jana told her friends who lived in the border settlement that she had been offered the chance to go to our school. There were many other children there who, like her, had no access to education. On the first morning that our tuk-tuk driver dropped Jana off at Sokhem, he delivered exciting news for the other children at the border region as well. Soon they would all have the same opportunity to attend school along with Jana.

The Sokhem Village campus shows innovation at its finest, when new solutions are found to change lives for the better. The human mind is so powerful, isn't it? Its infinite creativity gives hope that even the most difficult problems our world faces can one day be solved.

Every day at our schools in rural Cambodia, we're encouraging children, including those living in the hardest situations, that their minds and ideas matter. For when imagination is encouraged, and children gain the vital knowledge that they are seen, heard, and valued…the results can be transformative.

The Heart of Community

Chapter 5: Collaboration

Harmony will only come to the world when we agree to join hands for the common good.

David Zhang, LWB-China Team Member

    One clear lesson from the global pandemic in 2020 is that, whether or not people want to admit it, we are all in this together. The only way to overcome a virus that is ravaging the entire world is for countries, health agencies, and a whole host of others to collaborate in the best way possible. Cooperation is something we start teaching our children from the earliest age possible, isn't it? Turn on *Sesame Street* during pretty much any episode, and there will be Elmo or Big Bird encouraging kids to share, take turns, and work together to solve problems. As we get older, however, those kindergarten lessons on cooperation often start to fade, as competition and striving to be #1 take center stage. Thankfully, in the work that LWB gets to do each day, we see firsthand that collaboration can bring out the very best in all of us.

In early 2017, right after we began our work in Uganda, we received an email from a father who was desperately searching for help for his baby boy:

> *I am Ronald Ssejjuuko, Ugandan by nationality. I have a baby son called Kaniel born with a Truncus Arteriosus Type 1. I was advised by Doctors at Uganda Heart Institute to take him outside Uganda for open heart surgery as soon as possible. But I do not have the money needed. Can your esteemed organization help, so that I can save the life of my only son?*

To give you some perspective on the cardiac situation in this East African region, there is only one heart surgery hospital in the entire country of Uganda. The Uganda Heart Institute is able to do quality repairs for less complicated heart conditions like ASD and VSD but cannot take on more complex cases. In Uganda, it is estimated that 15,000 babies a year are born with heart defects. Of these, 8,000 a year need surgery to survive, and yet less than 1,000 receive the medical help they need. Back in 2017, when Kaniel's father first wrote to us, the entire country of Uganda had just four cardiologists.

We immediately wrote back to Ronald to ask for his son's medical records and then began contacting overseas children's hospitals. We needed someone to say "yes" as quickly as possible so Kaniel would not miss his short window of opportunity to have his heart healed. Arranging international medical care can often take many months, as the doctors and hospitals must first agree on a care plan before sending it to their charity committees for final approval. Sometimes just getting a medical visa or passport issued so a child can leave the country can take an extended period of time.

As our team began reaching out to heart surgeons in the US, we also reached out to two organizations who had a long history of helping children born with heart defects. Save a Child's Heart and the House of Destiny had already collaborated with LWB in the past to provide heart surgery for an orphaned boy in China named Lucas.

Back in 2012, LWB had been contacted by an orphanage in eastern China about a little boy in their care whose lips were a deep blue. He had a very complex heart defect that should have been repaired in infancy; yet somehow, he had survived in the orphanage to the age of 4. His fingers were clubbed from a continual lack of oxygen, but his curiosity sure wasn't dampened in any way. We sent Lucas to one of the top heart hospitals in Shanghai so that a diagnostic heart cath could be done. I think everyone on the ward knew his name by the end of the day as the only time he wasn't exploring was when he was fast asleep.

Unfortunately, the heart cath showed that Lucas' pulmonary artery was so severely impacted that surgery in China would not be possible. His orphanage director, after speaking with the doctors, accepted the diagnosis that Lucas was inoperable. She returned with Lucas to their home province with a heavy heart.

The LWB team kept searching for answers, however, and we were thrilled when Save a Child's Heart in Israel agreed to accept Lucas for the complicated surgery. Our medical manager in China then had the difficult task of convincing local officials to grant formal approval for Lucas to fly all the way to Israel for a very high-risk operation. With each new legal consent form I would send to China for the orphanage to sign, our medical director would write back and say, "You have to be kidding me."

Since Lucas did end up having a successful surgery in Israel and has long since met his permanent family through adoption, I can now share that there are awful considerations that must be discussed when sending a child overseas for surgery. What if a child dies in another country? What steps would be needed to return a body home? I really thought the whole surgery plan for Lucas was going to fall through at the last minute when the orphanage needed to sign a "repatriation of remains" form since his surgery carried so much risk. No orphanage director ever wants to do something to bring negative government attention to their facility, and having to get approval from higher-ups to potentially fly a coffin back is a risk that very few officials would be willing to take. Somehow our director got that paper signed, and Lucas then headed to Israel for the surgery which saved his life.

Several years later, when we received the letter from Kaniel's father in Uganda, we immediately wondered if the exact same multi-charity collaboration could help a young baby in Uganda as well. I'm happy to share that just like Lucas, Kaniel was accepted for heart surgery at Wolfson Children's Hospital in Israel. His operation was also a wonderful success. It only happened because different organizations around the world all came together with a singular purpose. Each of us had a part to play in providing the logistics, funding, and surgery skills needed to make sure another precious child got his second chance at life.

In February 2020, I was finally able to meet little Kaniel for the first time in person, along with his kind and humble parents, Ronald and Joy. As I sat in their Ugandan home one beautiful Sunday afternoon, I finally heard the full story of just how miraculous their son's healing truly was.

Ronald shared that late one evening in July 2016 baby Kaniel made his long-awaited entrance into the world. The midwife soon handed the tiny boy to Ronald while saying, "Now dedicate your child to God." Ronald lifted little Kaniel high in the air and said a special prayer for his son's life. The joy in the room was immense.

Just a few short hours later, however, Kaniel went into distress. His breathing became labored, and the nurses came running to whisk the tiny baby away to the ICU. Ronald said it was so awful to see his newborn son connected to machines, with no one being able to explain exactly what was happening to his first-born child. The great joy in the new parents' hearts turned to a deep, aching pain.

When the doctor finally came to speak with them, he delivered the difficult news that Kaniel had been born with a very complex heart defect, stating, "He should not be able to live even a single day." Ronald said he felt a strong sense of peace come over him, however. He looked at his little boy and told the medical team, "It is well...it is well. I know God has a plan for my son." The doctor replied, "You can continue to believe God, but I still need to tell you that your son's heart will fail without immediate surgery."

Baby Kaniel was soon discharged from the hospital, with no hope of being healed in Uganda. When the family returned home, new mother Joy told her husband that she had decided to fast for 40 days to ask God to help their child. Ronald stopped at this point in his story, smiling wide with the memory of his wife's faith. He then shared his immediate response to his wife. "You just gave birth, Joy. You cannot fast. You must eat and rest, or I'm afraid you will die."

Joy quietly replied, "If I die... let me die, but we need an answer from God about our child."

Ronald knew he had to be strong for his wife. He said that any time he felt like crying about his son's failing health, he would go into another room so she wouldn't see his deep sadness while her own heart was so broken. He would cry for his son, wipe the tears from his eyes, and then come back out to assure his wife that "all would be well."

As they both began their fast, Ronald began contacting heart hospitals he found online. He told me how painful it was to receive one email from India that read, "You just need to let your son go. His heart is too complicated. Just let him pass away." Another hospital in Canada replied that Kaniel would not survive infancy with his complex anatomy. The doctor wrote that continuing to search for help was only a waste of time. That certainly wasn't the news that Ronald and Joy were praying to hear.

On day 12 of their fasting, early in the morning around 7 am, Ronald told me he was praying when he heard a clear voice say, "Love Without Boundaries." (Yes, every hair on my arms stood up at this point). He even looked around the room for the person who spoke the words as he was completely alone at that time. He thought that perhaps God was speaking to his heart about His unfailing love, so Ronald began searching his Bible for any supporting scriptures. He was not able to find those exact three words in anything he read, though.

Ronald then turned to the Internet to see what he might be able to find online. He typed "Love Without Boundaries" into the Google search bar, and thank goodness our website came up first! He sat staring at the computer screen looking at our website, feeling a bit amazed that the three words he'd heard earlier that morning just happened to be a children's charity. He immediately sent a message to our LWB email address.

Within an hour, Ronald had our first reply, which he said filled his heart with new hope for his son. Soon after, Kaniel flew to Israel for the surgery which saved his life, and three years later I got to sit in Uganda and watch this incredible little boy run around his home nonstop.

When Ronald shared the full story of how his son's healing came to be, it honestly took my breath away. I continually ask God if we are on the right path. Are we doing everything we can to help the children who need us? Are we staying true to our core belief that Every Child Counts? Hearing Ronald's story was such a powerful encouragement to my heart that we have to keep going, no matter the obstacles, because so many more Kaniels are out there still waiting.

I wasn't the only one who got to hear the extraordinary story of how little Kaniel was healed, however. Some of my favorite parts about doing this work for so long are the moments when we see the help given by LWB to one child go on to impact another. It's like that beautiful analogy of a pebble being dropped in the water whose ripples go on to touch ever-widening circles. Those moments frequently catch me completely by surprise, but they've helped me realize fully that you can never know how a single act of kindness for one person can go on to impact another life forever.

News of Kaniel's healing began to spread in Uganda as people shared his remarkable story. A family from another part of the country heard rumors of a little boy born with a "broken heart" who had somehow survived and grown stronger. This family had received the same devastating news that their 3-year-old daughter, Rachael, had been born with such complex heart defects that she could never be healed in Uganda. Rachael had struggled since birth with her oxygen levels, and her weakened state caused her to be hospitalized many times with malaria, pneumonia, and then measles. Each time, she somehow found the strength to recover, but her mother knew that her health was continuing to decline.

Even though it was a very long distance from her home, Rachael's mother decided to make the trek to find the "boy who lived" and see for herself the child who miraculously found healing. Once she met Kaniel's family and learned that strangers around the world had helped him, she was filled with hope for her daughter. Ronald wrote us once again by email, this time asking if we could possibly find help for little Rachael. As soon as we heard her story, we began working to find a way for her heart to be healed as well.

One of our wonderful volunteers in the US had a connection to the Mayo medical center in Minnesota; soon Rachael's medical records were being studied by their cardiovascular department. The heart surgeons at Mayo felt that even though her heart defect was extremely complex, there was still a window of opportunity for her to undergo surgery. Just a few months later, Rachael and her mother boarded their first airplane flight to head to the US for heart surgery. One more pebble of goodness dropped into the water. One more beautiful child's life saved.

In 2019, LWB gained the wonderful blessing of having Joy and Ronald Ssejjuuko agree to become the directors of LWB-Uganda. As new heart cases come our way, Joy and Ronald handle all the in-country logistics. And because they have lived through the emotional journey themselves, there is no one better equipped to reassure each anxious parent about what is truly involved when a child undergoes heart surgery.

I want to share one additional story of those ripples in the water that illustrates just how much good can be done when even complete strangers take the time to care. In early 2020, we learned about a toddler in Uganda who had been born with multiple medical needs. Almost immediately after birth, tiny Rae was whisked away from her mom to undergo an emergency operation for anal atresia.

Days later, she was diagnosed with a complex heart issue as well — an atrioventricular (AV) canal defect. This condition involves a large hole in the very center of the heart chambers, along with faulty valves. Without surgery, Rae's heart would eventually fail.

Upon hearing this news, Rae's father deserted his wife and newborn daughter. Sadly, it is not uncommon for mothers and children in Uganda to be abandoned after a difficult medical diagnosis. Overwhelmed and now completely on her own, Rae's mom, Lydia, had to carry the full weight of navigating her daughter's medical crisis. Even as she struggled to pay for the most minimal food and shelter, she knew she couldn't give up trying to save the life of her baby girl.

One day, Lydia found an old, discarded megaphone that she realized could amplify her voice. She began pleading on the streets for people to help her daughter. Each day she moved from place to place, begging through the megaphone for funds which could help get her daughter the medical care she needed. Despite being truly exhausted walking all day to each new region, she told us that she only had to look at Rae's sweet face to know she could not give up.

One lonely day, however, after counting the meager funds she had gathered, Lydia came to the sobering realization that she would never be able to raise enough money to pay for her daughter's heart surgery.

Even with that anguish, she refused to surrender. She walked wearily to the heart hospital and once again raised the megaphone to her mouth. Instead of asking for funding, however, she began pleading for the names of any charities that were helping children in Uganda.

Then something absolutely wonderful happened. LWB had recently provided heart surgery for a little girl named Mia. At the exact moment that Lydia was crying out to the universe that she needed a charity to help her daughter live, Mia's mom walked by. It was a meeting made in heaven.

Mia's mom shared with Lydia that her daughter's surgery had been arranged by Love Without Boundaries. She had Joy and Ronald's cell number saved in her phone. She quickly pulled up the contact information and wrote their number down on a small scrap of paper.

Lydia, who just moments before had felt such a heavy weariness that no one seemed to care about her daughter's life, now had LWB's phone number clenched tightly in her hand. Within days, we had little Rae's medical file being evaluated by specialists, and soon after she was accepted for surgery by Narayana Hospital in Kolkata, India.

We were so grateful to our wonderful supporters when Rae's surgery was fully funded. Everything was falling perfectly into place for Rae to finally get the heart surgery she needed. Passports were issued and airline tickets arranged. Rae and her mom were standing at the Indian embassy in Uganda in early March 2020, waiting to pick up their medical visas, when the news came down that international airports around the world were closing immediately due to COVID-19.

In an instant, Lydia's dream of saving her daughter's life was suddenly put on hold.

To say it was an excruciating eight-month wait would be an understatement, but we never gave up hope. We regularly checked in with Rae's mom, reassuring her that the LWB community was praying continually for her daughter. We also provided nutritional support during the lockdown to keep Rae as strong as possible. We tried our best to give Lydia the much-needed peace that she and her daughter would be on their way to India for the long-anticipated surgery the moment Uganda's airport was open once again for business.

In November 2020, the day Rae's mom had longed for finally arrived when the Uganda airport reopened for international flights. This inseparable duo then took their very first airplane ride all the way from East Africa to India.

Following a host of exams and in-depth consultations, darling Rae was cleared to undergo surgery. She received her life-saving heart operation on November 20th, and we all cheered loudly when she was able to come off the ventilator just a few hours later. By the very next day, she was already able to take a few bites of food. Within days, Rae was so full of new energy that we joked that her mom was sure going to have her hands full keeping up with her. What a wonderful challenge to have!

Rae and Lydia's story illustrates so clearly how keeping hope in our hearts can sustain us. Even during her own darkest hours, abandoned and alone, Rae's mom continued to fight for her daughter's life, clinging to the hope that someone would finally hear her plea. I am grateful that, while so many others had simply hurried by, the person who finally listened to the tired mom with a megaphone was another parent touched by LWB.

With each new child accepted into our medical program, the circle of heart families in Uganda continues to grow and strengthen. I love seeing that whenever we post a new child who needs surgery on our Facebook or Instagram pages, the parents of the Ugandan children already healed always write such heartfelt messages of caring and support. They celebrate the children we heal in other countries as well, because they understand so profoundly that love has no boundaries when it comes to a child's life. In this big and often messy world, there's so much comfort to be found in being part of a welcoming community. When we take the time to listen and encourage one another…whether in person, online, and yes, even through a megaphone…that's when real possibilities unfold.

The network we've developed over the years to help children receive surgery, both domestically and internationally, is a great example of LWB's commitment to actively seek out collaboration. Sometimes in life, however, we need to cooperate together even when we don't initially feel it's necessary.

From 2003 to 2016, our programs in China were running full speed ahead. We'd built an amazing system of healing for children from the orphanages with which we worked. Whenever they would receive a newly abandoned baby with medical needs, they would call LWB for help, and we'd quickly whisk the child away to a top hospital for treatment. Prior to and following their surgeries and hospital stays, they would come to live in one of our specialized healing homes, created especially for orphaned children to gain strength both before and after medical care. Upon graduating from the healing home, a child would then enter one of our many foster care locations, where they would grow up in a family until chosen for adoption. We had repeated this cycle almost a thousand times. Without a doubt, it was a system that worked beautifully for the kids.

In 2016, China passed a new foreign charity law which threw everything we were doing into enormous uncertainty. All foreign charities would now need to register with the Public Security Bureau, China's national police authority, and they also had to find a government supervisory organization that would be willing to oversee all activities done in the country.

For the next 18 months, I worked with our team in China to come into full compliance with the new laws. It was an extremely daunting task, with mountains of paperwork and endless meetings that caused many foreign groups to decide it just wasn't worth it. Since the law was so new, many government agencies didn't want to be one of the first to agree to sponsor an international organization. Orphanages were not allowed to be sponsors, and most of our work was done at the local level. I'll just say I know how door-to-door salesmen must feel as we sure had a lot of doors slammed in our face.

In late 2017, however, Love Without Boundaries received our national certificate to continue our important work for children after signing a cooperation agreement with the Anhui Health Commission. I think our shouts of jubilation must have registered on all the seismological monitors around the world when the final red stamp of approval was issued. Our joy was coupled with a growing sense of sorrow, however, as many of the wonderful foreign charities we had worked with for years had begun closing their operations after not being able to find a government partner. It was absolutely heartbreaking to see the children in their care have to return back to their orphanages.

For the next year, our LWB programs continued without any interruptions. At that point in time, we had been providing foster care in China for 14 years, supporting family-based care for thousands of orphaned children across 26 different cities. We had just inked the deal on a new foster care project with an orphanage in northern China as well.

However, we all know that life can change dramatically in the blink of an eye. Late one night, my phone rang with a call from our director in China. I then had to face the sad reality that even with formal registration, our work with orphaned children was about to change in a major way.

When it comes to the evolution of orphan care in China over the last two decades, the country deserves a lot of recognition for the massive amount of funding they've invested into several national projects for abandoned children. Their programs for providing medical care and education have improved the lives of thousands of kids living in government orphanages.

However, one recent facet of orphan care in China I find concerning is the return to a system of institutionalism. A global body of evidence showing that children develop best in families has led to a commitment by most countries around the world to move away from care in residential facilities. Foster care is often a child's only chance to experience life outside an institution's locked gates, and LWB was providing truly individualized care to the orphaned children we placed in local families. I had never met a single good-hearted orphanage director who hadn't privately agreed that the children raised with loving foster parents did far better developmentally than the children who stayed in the institution.

In cities all across China, however, new policies and liability concerns are causing the rapid demise of a once vibrant foster care system. I am extremely saddened by this shift, as I believe well implemented foster care in local communities should be a vital part of any country's plan for its vulnerable children.

In China, while we were 100% committed to keeping all the children in LWB care with their dedicated foster parents for as long as needed, a shift in opinions at several government levels had indeed changed everything in an instant. Our director had phoned me that late summer evening to share the terrible news that new policies were being implemented which required all orphaned children living with foster families to be returned to institutional care. Many orphanage officials, not wanting to do anything to jeopardize their jobs, had decided the children needed to be moved back immediately. In some cities where we worked, the families were given just a few hours' notice, breaking the hearts of not only the children suddenly thrust back into unfamiliar orphanages but their devoted foster parents as well.

One of the children in LWB foster care impacted by this enormous change was little Benji. In 2015, representatives from an adoption agency had visited his meager orphanage. They had called us immediately after returning to let us know that this 7-month-old baby born with Down syndrome needed urgent intervention. The first photos I saw showed that he looked more like a newborn. His furrowed brow and skinny arms were difficult to see. Of course, we agreed to do whatever we could to find out why he was failing to thrive. His orphanage allowed us to move him urgently to the hospital for medical exams and IV nutrition.

The testing we did showed that Benji was unable to process normal formula due to a severe allergy, so his body had become extremely weak and malnourished. Due to his compromised state, he developed a severe infection and high fevers. Benji was an extremely sick little boy, but he continued to cling to life in the hospital.

Over the next few days, Benji began to stabilize. Although at first he didn't like his new synthetic formula, his appetite soon improved, and he grew stronger with each passing day. He was then able to be discharged from the hospital to one of our healing homes, where our nannies got to work helping him put on the pounds to remove the worried wrinkles from his forehead. I sure wish I could show you Benji's before and after photos because, by the time he graduated from our healing home into LWB foster care, he looked like an absolute Gerber baby. I remember visiting his foster home one day and laughing as I bent down to pick him up, as "Moose Baby" didn't do him justice. This boy was a CHUNK. I joked with his foster mom about her strong biceps from carrying him up and down the many flights of apartment stairs. He was happy, healthy, and ready for a forever home.

Sadly, even after Benji's adoption paperwork was filed the following year, no one had yet stepped forward. It was then that we got the crushing phone call in 2018 that foster care was no longer allowed in his province. Benji had to say goodbye to the only parents he had known for the last two and a half years to move back inside an enormous institution. We were devastated because we knew that orphanage life is often a real struggle for children with Down syndrome. And we were not wrong. Benji was moved to a floor in the orphanage for children with severe special needs and went back to his early life when he could only lie in his crib looking at the ceiling. He became thin and shut down, and, in his grief over losing his foster parents, he began banging his head on his crib walls as well.

Shortly after foster care was stopped in most provinces in China, further regulations were put into place saying orphaned children could not be cared for anywhere outside government buildings. This, of course, was going to have huge ramifications for our healing homes program. LWB (just like almost every other orphan charity in China) was caring for children in privately rented homes and apartments. It seemed as if no organization would be given an exemption, as even the most well-known charities working to care for medically fragile, orphaned children began receiving the news that all of their kids would have to move back to their home institutions. It was gut-wrenching.

While LWB had not yet received any official notifications, we knew we had to be proactive in figuring out a way to keep the fragile children safely in our care. About a year before, we had been approached by a new government PT hospital that was open to a partnership. But since the majority of our medical work involved surgeries, we had not explored this further. As healing homes throughout China began having to close their doors, we knew it was time to call a meeting to see how we might collaborate for the kids.

I now know it had been short-sighted of me to not consider a move to the PT hospital earlier, but we loved the "real home" feeling that our healing home apartments gave to the children. The babies would zoom from one room to another in their walkers, while the toddlers would walk down the apartment stairwell with their nannies to play at the neighborhood park. I always loved visiting our homes in China because they were such warm and happy places for the children to recover. The new government policies had forced our hand, however. We now had urgent work in front of us to build a strong relationship with the PT hospital so we could create a secure and impactful project together to help orphaned children.

Thankfully, the new healing home location has allowed us to continue our important work in helping children who need specialized care. We moved into the new facility in August 2019, after being given a wing of the therapy center which we were allowed to remodel. Despite being inside a hospital, we've created a home-like environment, complete with a family room, bedrooms, and a big playroom. Because this project is in an approved government facility, we can now move children from even more orphanages without issue.

In addition, by cooperating with the PT hospital and sharing the responsibility of this important project, we've seen that the children definitely benefit as well. Now every child we move to our healing home has daily therapy services on site. Whether it's a child with cleft needing formalized speech therapy or a baby with CP who needs strengthening exercises to help their mobility, this partnership has added another essential piece of bringing real healing to orphaned children with special needs.

There was another wonderful benefit of formalizing this new collaboration. It allowed us to bring children who had been part of our foster care program before it was closed back into our hands. We all hoped and prayed that little Benji could be one of them.

When we were finally given permission to move Benji to the new location of our China Healing Home, he had been back in his orphanage for an entire year. The first reports from our nannies were difficult to hear. He was extremely solemn and refused to make eye contact. One nanny said, "No matter how hard you tried, he simply wouldn't see you at all."

Thankfully, our nannies are used to institutionalized children coming into their care who need extra assurance and support. Even though he was now 4 years old, Benji wasn't able to eat solid food when he returned to us, and so the nannies simply began bottle feeding him again. He wanted to just sit in the corner of his crib and bump his head against the rails, so they put him in a high chair in the middle of the playroom, allowing him to see all the people around him and get to know the flow of the home.

Slowly...slowly...he finally agreed to be held. And then he felt safe enough to look into his nanny's eyes.

You might have heard our huge celebration several months later when he gave a first small smile, and then, a few days later, a low chuckle was definitely heard as well. Soon Benji began to play with the other children in the home, and our hearts were full when he started showing comfort and love to the younger babies in his room by holding their hands or sharing a toy. I knew it was still extremely fragile, but his little heart had once again begun to bloom.

Benji had lived through so many hard things in the four short years he had been on the earth. The enormous loss of his birth parents would have been difficult enough to bear. But then, because of an undiagnosed allergy, he spent months slowly starving, as the regular and soy formulas the orphanage tried only made him more ill.

He then knew real joy in our healing home and foster care, only to have his caregivers disappear once more in an instant. In his grief – his raw and understandable grief – the only way he could cope was to withdraw.

Benji is why we can never stop advocating for orphaned children to find permanency. **Every child born needs a family.** Every child needs that one devoted person who will always be there for them, to comfort them when they are grieving and to come running in times of need. The reality is that no matter how wonderful a charity's programs are for an orphaned child, they are all just temporary and subject to change in an instant if a new regulation comes to pass.

I want Benji to have his forever, officially legal Mama Bear. I want Benji to know that a caring, permanent family will always be there for him. I want that for every orphaned child staying in our healing home, because I know that at some point those precious children will have to leave our care. I pray each and every day that when that time comes, it will be into the arms of a loving mom or dad instead of back to grow up in an institution. But for now, and for as long as we have permission, LWB will stand in the gap to make sure every child in our care feels protected, nurtured, and loved.

The Heart of Community

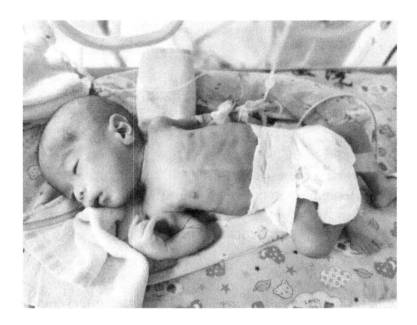

Chapter 6: Compassion

Compassion is a virtue of the heart, driven by love. It allows us to step outside of ourselves and see the circumstances of others. Compassion is more than emotion; it is a core attribute of servanthood. It makes us better people than we ever dreamed we could be and makes our existence meaningful and worthwhile.

Ronald Ssejjuuko, LWB-Uganda Director

    When my son Patrick was a senior in high school, he flew to Nashville by himself for a college visit. I wasn't too worried about sending him on his own as his older brother was already attending college there. It was supposed to be a quick three-day weekend, but then I got the awful news that no parent ever wants to hear. Patrick had been severely injured in an accident and was being rushed to Vanderbilt University with a head injury.

I honestly don't remember very much about how I got to the Oklahoma City airport, but I remember running to the airline counter and telling the young man working there that I had to get on the next flight to Tennessee. I know I was a mess, telling him through my tears that my son was in a medically induced coma and was alone in the ICU. It would have been so easy for the airline employee to just issue the ticket and send me on my way…but he didn't do that. Instead, he put his hand over my own, asked me the name of my son, and then reached for the microphone on the airport PA system.

> *Can I have everyone's attention please? This mom just learned that her son Patrick is in a coma in Nashville, and she needs to get to him as quickly as she can. Can everyone please take a moment to say a prayer for her son Patrick Eldridge… that he will receive all the medical care needed to be restored to full health.*

For a few unexpected moments, everyone in the Oklahoma City airport was silent, lifting prayers for my son. It was such a beautiful moment of compassion between complete strangers, and I carried the sense of peace it brought to my heart all the way to my son's hospital bedside. I remember feeling so grateful that day to be part of the Oklahoma community, and I will always remember that young man at the airport who took the time to care.

In the work I do each day with vulnerable children, I think a lot about the word "compassion." I believe it's such an essential element of authentic charity work. I've actually read about the origin of the word, which comes from the Old French *compassioun*, literally meaning "a suffering with another." The key part to me of that precise definition is the word WITH. Sincere compassion involves connection. It isn't pity, which is often associated with a sense of superiority. Pity can sometimes feel like, *"Oh poor you,"* while secretly harboring *"I'm sure glad it's not me."* Compassion arises deeper in our hearts as a sincere response to another person's sorrow. It requires us to pay attention to those around us and not simply walk by. When the young employee took my hand that day in the airport after seeing my grief over my son's accident, his simple action said, *"I see you. I hear you. And I'm sorry you're in pain."*

There isn't a single day that goes by in my work with LWB that I don't get to see the profound impact that can occur when our hearts "suffer with another." When we cultivate compassion, in both ourselves and our community, our desire for action then grows.

———

LWB has always tried to bring help to children by connecting with people in the local community who already know the area and understand the greatest needs. It has been incredible over the years to see a vast, invisible network be knit together of passionate people connected through kindness. It has allowed us to help children living in regions that are often more difficult to access, and it has allowed us to provide medical care for those in even the most remote villages. It was in one such village, along the Himalayan mountain range on the Tibetan plateau, where we were first introduced by a local team member to 7-year-old Ema.

Ema and her family lived in a mountain area filled with forests and rivers, at what was described to me as "lower elevation" since it was only at 9,000 feet! In the spring, the hillsides were covered with peach blossoms as far as the eye could see. In the winter, however, the snows could be brutal, cutting off transportation often from October to April. Ema's father tried to support the family by finding odd jobs whenever he could and by picking matsutake mushrooms each summer along the forest floors. He told us that he and his wife were overjoyed when their first daughter Ema had been born.

Just two days after she arrived into the world, however, they knew something was terribly wrong. Just like Ollie, whom I wrote about earlier, Ema had been born with an anorectal malformation needing immediate surgery. Ema's parents took her to the nearest doctor, but he said he could not help the tiny baby, who was now in great pain. They were sent to a county hospital next, but the doctors there also stated that they couldn't possibly attempt the complex surgery little Ema needed. Finally, the weary parents took their daughter to the capital city of Lhasa, but even there the doctors said they wouldn't dare give Ema general anesthesia since she was just a baby. They told the family to come back when she was older, and they then would attempt the surgery she needed. Somehow, Ema survived the next long year of constant pain.

When Ema was 18 months old, the family again returned to Lhasa. In larger pediatric centers, a child with anal atresia would most likely receive one of two procedures, depending on the severity of the birth defect. Some children receive anoplasty, a reconstruction surgery allowing stool to pass normally. Others receive a temporary colostomy and then a follow-up surgery, to move a child's colon and create an anal opening. Ema received neither of those procedures. Instead, a large plastic tube was inserted into Ema's back side to drain her body's waste. While the tube managed to stay in place almost two years, it left Ema with serious complications. At age 7, she felt such acute pain whenever she had to use the bathroom that she often passed out completely.

When our local team member first met this sweet family, her heart was filled with compassion after hearing of Ema's continual suffering since birth. When she told the parents that LWB helped children receive medical care, their relief was immense. They explained that they had gone into debt over 25,000 rmb (almost $4,000 USD) trying to help their daughter and apologized for being a further burden to anyone. Ema's father said he thought they could possibly borrow another $1,000 if we would agree to help his child. We, of course, told him that our community would not want to see them go more into debt trying to heal little Ema. We could arrange for her to be seen by some of the top pediatric surgeons in Shanghai, but it would have to be done quickly before the looming heavy snows closed the village off for the winter.

The doctors in Shanghai told us Ema could be seen right away for her evaluation. It was decided that her father would travel with her since he knew a small bit of Mandarin, while her mom would stay behind. It would be a journey of over 3,000 miles.

A few days later, we received a frantic call from Ema's father. The only bridge in the region, allowing them to travel by bus to Lhasa to then catch a train to Shanghai, had collapsed from heavy rains. Local officials had said it could take a month (or longer) for it to be repaired, which would be too late to relieve Ema's pain. If she and her dad couldn't make it out of the region before October, the winter snows would stop her from getting the critical medical care she so desperately needed.

Parents often use the familiar adage that we would "move mountains" for our children, but for little Ema that is literally what her father decided must be done. Determined not to miss this opportunity to help his beloved daughter, he decided to hike by foot over the mountains to reach Lhasa. On many parts of the difficult, week-long journey, he had to carry Ema on his back.

By the time the humble family arrived in Shanghai, Ema and her dad were exhausted. Ema had only known the quiet countryside of her mountain home. Now she was in one of the largest children's hospitals in very crowded Shanghai, with doctors wanting to do immediate scans and medical exams, all speaking in a foreign tongue. She was understandably terrified, and even her father couldn't bring calm to her heart that first day in the big city. She clenched his hand tightly as the medical team finally decided to give her time to adjust to her new surroundings.

Within a day or two, Ema was like a different child. Our manager in Shanghai, Li Ping, told us she was already feeling relief from the medications she'd been given, and her outgoing personality was starting to peek through. Li Ping learned that Ema dreamed of going to school someday, and he assured her that, once the surgery was complete, she would finally have that opportunity.

The first test results showed what we already had feared. Years of not having access to medical care had caused extensive damage to Ema's intestines. She would need a bowel resection and colostomy before undergoing a second surgery in a few months' time. It would be impossible for Ema and her father to travel back to the Tibetan plateau during winter; so where would they stay between surgeries?

Enter the LWB Healing Homes Program, which up until this point had only cared for orphaned children with medical needs. We had never had a family stay before at the home, only babies and toddlers, but we knew we had to figure out a way to accommodate Ema and her father.

When we first approached her dad, asking if he'd be willing to travel several additional hours away to stay at our healing home while Ema recovered, it was honestly difficult for such a quiet, proud man to rely on charity once again. He said he'd only be willing if he could somehow make a contribution to our work. When we explained that the home was for babies who had been abandoned by their parents, he offered to help be their surrogate dad while he and Ema stayed in the home. We gladly accepted that deal.

Over the next few months, Ema was able to rest and recover beautifully. She really enjoyed being able to play big sister with all the babies in the home. Our nannies were well versed in her particular medical need, having cared for so many babies born with similar conditions, so they were able to teach both Ema and her father how to best manage her special need long-term. As Ema felt stronger, she and her dad were able to venture out into the city as tourists, seeing new sights and trying lots of new foods. What a huge adventure for a little girl who was now filled with laughter and smiles after finally becoming pain free.

Ema's second surgery was completely uneventful. Soon after, her doctors felt she had recovered fully and could now return home. Before leaving the hospital, Ema's father presented the physicians who had finally healed his daughter with a traditional Tibetan hada, a white silk scarf that symbolizes the highest respect and thanks given by the Tibetan people.

We were all going to miss darling Ema, but she had a mom back in her mountain village who was counting down the days until the family could be reunited. As we said our final goodbyes, we had one additional surprise for the family to help them well into the future. Our generous supporters gifted Ema and her parents with three pregnant female yaks, ensuring they would have not only milk and cheese for their own family's health but another income stream as well.

A few months later, we received updated photos from Ema's family. The yak calves had all been safely born, and in one image Ema was cuddling the shaggy babies whom she already dearly loved. My favorite photo, though, was of Ema's dad holding and twirling his daughter on a hillside, both laughing together in a moment of pure joy. While our chapter in Ema's life story had now come to a close, a brilliant future was clearly now in store.

―――――――――

The first night my son Patrick was in the Nashville ICU, the place felt almost hallowed, as if one needed to whisper the entire time since the babies and children were all so sick and fragile. I couldn't sleep at all that first night by his bedside. I just stared and watched the different machines and monitors to which he was connected, praying with each heartbeat that the bleeding in his brain would somehow miraculously go away. The first two rooms on the ICU hall we were in had tiny babies recovering from heart surgery, their chest wounds freshly closed, and their faces still covered by oxygen masks. The equipment was bigger than the babies, and I watched their anxious parents rubbing their legs and holding their small hands.

In the room next to my son's, however, there was a tiny baby who had been born to a mother who couldn't care for her. I don't know the details, but I know that, except for the nurses who came in to do vitals, the baby was alone the entire time I was there. The first night, as all the other babies and children slept, she wailed. She cried a frightened cry, one that said, "I'm alone and where is everyone?" – a cry that pierced my mama's heart and made me wish I could just go pick her up and rock her.

I didn't know the rules of an ICU and didn't know whether I was even allowed in her room, but finally at 3 am I tiptoed in and stood by her bed. What a fighter she was. I am sure many babies would have given up calling out long before, but she continued to cry, while hooked to tubes and monitors and electronic devices that glowed in the night. She was so tiny and fragile, but I could tell she was strong in spirit. As I held one of her tiny fingers and said a prayer of comfort for her, I, of course, was transported in my mind to all the babies in orphanages who cry out in the night as well.

I will never get used to the idea that so many children around the world are sick and in need. The numbers are too big to even take in, which is why I always try to encourage our LWB team to take it one child at a time. Every child we can help is important, but I have to be honest that it can be overwhelmingly hard to receive one desperate plea after another from orphanages and parents who have critically ill children and nowhere else to turn.

There is no worse feeling in the world than to have to say no to a child needing surgery; but sadly, there's no charity I've found with a constant stream of unlimited funds. That means very difficult decisions often must be made – which children will have their hearts healed, for example, and which are turned away. When an orphanage or anguished parent sends photos of their sick child attached to the medical records, we often want to put our heads down on our desks to weep at the injustices surrounding access to healthcare.

Every child born deserves a chance to LIVE, but a system to give every child that chance still does not exist in our world. My family was one of the lucky ones. Insurance made it possible for my son Patrick to get all the medical care he needed to recover from his head injury. For hundreds of thousands of children right this very moment, however, it's a sobering reality that their only chance at life depends on the compassion of strangers.

On a cold winter night at the end of 2019, a newborn baby was left outside on his own. We will probably never know the reasons why he was abandoned, but the little boy was in critical condition, struggling to breathe. The orphanage assigned to his case called us immediately, and we quickly had baby Trevor moved to a provincial children's hospital. There, tests confirmed what we could already see in pictures…Trevor's life hung in the balance. In addition to having severe pneumonia, which kills more children each year than any other infectious disease (an estimated 800,000 children annually), Trevor also had septicemia, one of the diagnoses I dread the most in fragile newborns. I have sadly seen far too many babies pass away after their blood is poisoned by circulating bacteria. A few hours later, Trevor's shallow breathing stopped. He was quickly placed on a ventilator, and, for the next 12 days, we didn't know whether he would survive.

In late January 2020, Trevor was finally able to take some tentative first breaths again on his own. His lungs remained extremely fragile. At the same time, we began hearing an increasing amount of news about a new virus that was spreading quickly through eastern China. Everything was so unknown, with rumors flying on social media. Was it the flu? Was it truly deadly? And of course, with our work, were children being impacted?

We began researching everything we could find online about the new virus given the name of COVID-19, as fear gripped all our team members in China. Our questions about how to best protect the children in our care continued to mount. Was it safer for Trevor to remain in the ICU where he could be potentially exposed by another patient, or would it be better for him to be discharged to one of our healing homes? The answer was soon taken out of our hands as the Chinese government began sealing off entire regions, with no one allowed to travel in or out. Tiny Trevor was now stranded in the ICU, and none of us at the time had any idea just how long this new virus would be around.

The hospital where Trevor was staying was designated a COVID facility later that week, and the doctors told us they felt the safest place Trevor could be was in the now sealed-off pediatric ICU. There would, of course, be a cost, however, as every day in the NICU came at a far higher price than being cared for on the regular hospital ward. Knowing that Trevor's medical bills were about to skyrocket substantially, we reached out to our supporters to let them know this small, orphaned baby needed people in his corner.

I am so grateful that our community wrapped their arms firmly around little Trevor, allowing him to stay in the safety of the NICU during the initial unknowns of the COVID pandemic. It changed everything for him. One day in late February, his oxygen levels dropped to just 50%, and his skin became deathly pale. More testing showed he was critically anemic and had developed necrotizing enterocolitis (NEC), a severe inflammation of his intestines. As his abdomen began to fill with fluid, we once again had to face the possibility that this little baby could pass away without ever knowing what it felt like to be loved in a family.

Somehow Trevor found the strength to keep fighting. February turned to March, and then April into May. While COVID raged around him just outside the ICU doors, Trevor continued his own private battle to survive. He received several blood transfusions and needed almost continual oxygen assistance. Our supporters never gave up hope, however, and each time we needed more funding for his hospital stay, another kind person stepped forward to help him.

In June, Trevor was finally well enough to stay full-time in our healing home. He had beaten all the odds, going from being left outside in frigid temperatures as a newborn to now being held gently in our loving nannies' arms. Trevor embraced life outside the hospital incubator with a newfound gusto, downing his bottles in record time and accepting his breathing treatments happily as long as he could look up with contentment into his caregiver's eyes.

Trevor is now such a perfect picture of health that no one meeting him for the first time would ever know how perilously close he came to dying far too soon. When I look at his adorable photos, it is difficult to consider that if a charity wouldn't have agreed to fund his emergency medical care, he would have been yet another statistic, an orphaned child quietly cremated and thrown away. Would anyone have remembered him or truly mourned if he had simply passed away?

I am thankful that we don't have to dwell on that question when it comes to gorgeous Trevor. Kind-hearted people, who most likely will never meet him in person, heard his story and decided to take action. Trevor's young life was saved. I can't wait for the day that he is chosen for adoption and his new family can then be the ones mooning over his sweet, engaging grin.

I wish more than anything that I could somehow take away the sorrows of how Trevor's journey on this earth began. No baby should ever have to endure so much pain and awful uncertainty, but there's no magic wand that allows us to erase it. As he grows, I know Trevor will have to process the difficult things he went through after being left all on his own in such a fragile condition. I pray that someday there might be a sense of peace in his heart from knowing just how many people cared about his life as a baby. The sad truth is that the only reason any of us need compassion in our lives is because suffering is a part of it. We can find comfort, however, in reminding ourselves that while our world is indeed a broken place, it is also filled with the immeasurable power of love.

When I was in fifth grade, I had a deeply spiritual moment that I still remember vividly. I was sitting in class listening to my teacher when I suddenly became acutely aware that my heart was beating and my lungs were breathing. It was as if I could even feel my blood circulating through every vein and artery in my body. I sat at my desk feeling completely overwhelmed with the absolute miracle of being fully alive, and I looked around at my classmates in awe, knowing that each of their beating hearts was a perfect miracle as well. It was the first moment I can remember deeply understanding the true fragility of human life, as it washed over me that everything could stop in an instant if even one body system shut down.

I wish I could say that when I announced this newfound awareness to my teacher that she joined in my divine enthusiasm, but I could tell pretty quickly she was instead quietly thinking to herself, "Amy, you are so weird." I learned to keep my reverence for how extraordinary human life is to myself as a child, but I never stopped marveling. I'm grateful that as an adult I can talk much more openly about it, although now it's my children who are probably quietly thinking to themselves, "Mom, you are so weird."

I only bring up this story because I hope it helps show why compassion has always been such a vitally important part of the culture of LWB. I've never lost that wonder that every person on this earth is a living, breathing miracle. How fortunate I feel to work each day with people who share that same deep respect for humanity. Think of the societal changes that could happen if we all looked at each other with a little bit of awe, realizing that we're supposed to be equal as humans, not above or below. We all enter the world crying and completely vulnerable, immediately needing others if we hope to survive. Somewhere along the way, we lose that sense of vulnerability, even viewing it as a sign of weakness.

Practicing compassion connects us again to each other and reminds us that every human is equally worthy of being loved and understood. It allows us to admit that we really do need each other, sharing our sorrows without fear of being judged and then reaching out to others when they are the ones in pain. I think it lets the best part of our humanity shine through.

In 2016, I once again saw the unlimited power of compassion when Leng, LWB's selfless director in Cambodia, told me he wanted to take me to the city landfill. I attempted a lame joke by saying something like, "Wow…you really know all the great places to take a lady," which was my poor attempt to hide my fears about what I knew we would most likely see. Leng had shared with me before I left the US that many children worked at the landfill, often for 14 or more hours a day. But I would soon learn that they actually live at the dumpsite as well. Nothing could have prepared me for what we were about to see.

We took motorcycles out to the landfill, and, as we drew closer, the smell of decay began to fill the air. By the time we pulled up to the actual site, the fumes from the sewage and decomposing waste were so intense that we wished we didn't have to breathe.

We walked down the dirt path into the dump in our sandals. As the wet, thick mud covered our feet, I realized we were picking up garbage as it stuck to our shoes: rotting food, medical waste bags, hypodermic needles. Trying to scrape the items off our sandals only caused more things to stick. As I kneeled down to pull off a wooden skewer that had gone under my shoe strap, I discovered that the dump was alive and moving with a blanket of maggots and worms, so I quickly stood back up. The smells and the sights were an assault on one's senses, but most sickening to me was the constant noise, as masses of black flies swarmed and hummed – so loudly that it seemed like the set of a horror film. It was hard to fully take in that everything around me was real.

Then, as we turned the corner down another aisle of garbage mountains... CHILDREN. Beautiful, amazing children, walking toward us to see their friend Leng. My heart shattered into a thousand different pieces.

We had stopped on the way to buy them some food, which the kids were definitely happy to see, but the older ones only paused for a moment to accept it before immediately returning to their work. This was their daily life, laboring through the entire night at times to escape the hottest temps. Leng told me they often work from 2 am until 7 am, digging through the mountains of garbage for recyclables they can gather and sell, and searching for food scraps to fill their empty stomachs.

I know everyone would agree that no child should have this life. No one deserves to live inside a landfill. Leng shared with us, though, that the parents feel working in the dump is far more honorable than begging on the streets, since they are at least earning their way. He went on to explain, however, that since the children didn't go to school, there could never be a better life. He shook his head with sadness, saying in a quiet voice, "Poverty is all they have known and all they will ever know."

One of the first little girls I met at the landfill was 8-year-old Mercy. She and her family lived at the dump site in a homemade shanty built from scraps of corrugated metal and boxes. Instead of grass, her backyard was filled with the dangers of medical and electronic waste, shards of glass, and rotting diapers.

As we approached, Mercy stopped digging through the garbage in front of her to shyly see what surprises we had brought. Her thin arms and legs looked like little sticks poking out from her well-worn red top and shorts. Mercy was so stunted in her physical growth that she looked like she was no more than 4 years old.

It was impossible to stand in the middle of that landfill and not ask myself the age-old question of why people are dealt different hands in life. Why had I been born to middle-class parents in a quiet suburb, where the biggest worry of my childhood was whether we'd make it home in time for dinner after an afternoon of playing, while Mercy...this beautiful, gentle little girl in front of me...had been born in a landfill instead? I struggle with this question more deeply with each passing year, after seeing the enormous inequities faced by children who live in hard places. I still haven't found a good answer, but I don't think God minds me asking, especially not after all the sad and unfair things the children we help have experienced and seen.

The unsolved question of fate really came to the forefront for me early on in my work with LWB when we were working in an orphanage that had a floor very few were allowed to enter. Even the elevator wouldn't stop there, in case a visitor ever got lost in the large complex. You could only reach it by going up the backstairs and then unlocking a big, rusted gate. I was allowed to visit one evening when one of the orphanage nannies reported that a child on the floor had become unresponsive. So, at around 11 pm one night, the door was finally unlocked for me, and I got to meet 40 children I had no idea even existed before.

Most of the children I saw that night had severe special needs, and it was very difficult to take in their meager surroundings. There was just one caregiver for all of the children, and it's simply not possible for a lone person to care for 40 kids with more complex medical needs. It was a heartbreaking few hours, but by the end of the night, we had convinced the director that two of the children should be brought down to the main floor. Both girls had mild cerebral palsy, which might have impacted their limbs but not their minds. They deserved so much more than life in a concrete room, as did every child on that floor.

Each time we would visit, we would beg for another child or two to be brought downstairs, and I know the director was astonished that every one of those children who left the hidden floor went on to be chosen by families. This was back in a time when there were often strict quotas on the number of children an orphanage could place for adoption. To this day, I still feel a deep sense of wrongfulness that our decisions to choose one child over another completely changed their futures. I know on the one hand I can look at those who "got out" and feel an immense joy that they escaped the gray cement room. But I will never forget all the others who were left behind after our visits. There is no way to ever come to terms with the unfairness of it all.

As I stood in the landfill for the first time in Cambodia, watching children comb through rotting mountains of trash, my questions on life's injustices returned again with a vengeance. Why is one child born into safety or comfort while another will know nothing but hardship along the way? Of course, I still haven't found an answer, but I've come to understand that recognizing all of us could have just as easily been born into such a different life is an essential step in developing profound compassion. When we admit that the scales of our birth, beyond any child's control, are often completely unbalanced, perhaps we can embrace one another with the deep respect that each human deserves.

Our director in Cambodia is one of those special people who has the innate ability to show respect and graciousness to others. Leng had brought us to the city dumpsite that day because for years he had wanted to come up with a way to help the children there escape what appeared to be a fate of continued poverty. He knew that education is one of the world's best equalizers, for knowledge is a gift that no one can ever take away. We had come to the landfill to see if any of the parents who lived there would allow their children to go to school if LWB sponsored their tuition.

That day, however, I quickly learned that when you are completely crippled by poverty, you can't even imagine a way out. The $1 a day recycling money your child makes, by finding hypodermic needle caps or plastic bottles among the sea of trash, seems like the difference between starving or feeding your family. On the day of my first visit to the landfill, Leng spoke to the parents with such quiet respect but was only able to convince one mother to send her two little boys to school.

There was no way he was giving up on those children, however. Over the next year, Leng returned regularly to the dumpsite, patiently explaining to the parents that their children deserved to learn to read and ever so slowly building their trust.

On the hot summer day I was next able to return, the flies swarmed so thickly that the landfill constantly hummed, literally shifting in sheets of black. It broke my heart once more to see little kids digging through the mounds of garbage with their bare hands. This time, however, I knew a lot more than I had before about the risk that children take by working inside a garbage site. I had read articles about children being buried alive by trucks unloading their waste. I found numerous case studies about the medical issues faced by kids in dumps, such as infected cuts from shards of metal or severe headaches and chronic respiratory issues from breathing in the gases released from burning garbage. Thankfully, Leng told us that the majority of parents now quietly wished for their children to somehow have a better life.

It had rained heavily just before we arrived at the dump. Walking through the site was now even more challenging as the decaying garbage mixed with the mud. Our sandals were sucked off almost instantly. As we got closer to the area where the children were, I realized that it was going to be next to impossible to cross one specific area to reach them, as it had essentially turned into a wet, contaminated bog. But then some of the fathers saw us coming, and they began grabbing bags of garbage to lay out like a carpet for us to walk on. One bag after another was thrown down across the mire to ensure us safe passage, which was both surreal and humbling at the exact same time.

The first child I saw up ahead was a little boy named Martin, whom I had met and photographed the year before as a toddler standing solemnly among the waste. Clad only in a well-worn shirt covered in stains, he remained quiet and somber on this visit as well, refusing to engage with Leng even after we tried to win him over with some little toys.

I quickly spied Mercy as well, standing timidly with the older children. She definitely looked one year older and was still as beautiful as ever. Her face was the one that I thought of each time we pledged to each other that we were not going to give up on getting all the children at the landfill enrolled in school someday. I was overjoyed on this trip when her mom was one of the very first parents to say YES. Mercy loves everything about going to school and has gone on to become an excellent student over the years.

By the end of 2020, we had enrolled almost 50 children from the landfill at our second LWB school campus in Rangsei Village. Each day, we send a large tuk-tuk to the dumpsite to pick up the children in the morning and then bring them safely home at night. The health of the children has changed so dramatically, as now they all get a nutritious hot lunch each day and regular check-ups by our medic. They also get eight hours where they learn to read, do math, skip rope, and play soccer. Eight hours each day that they don't breathe toxic fumes. I know it might seem like a small thing when you think about the enormous numbers of children around the world who still dig through dumpsites each day, but LWB's motto from the very beginning has been that Every Child Counts. For the 50 children at this one particular landfill in Cambodia, their lives count immensely.

Our work at the city dump has also allowed us to impact many other children as well, including the new babies born on site. When Leng visited the landfill one summer afternoon, he learned that one of the moms had recently delivered a little boy. The infant was struggling in a major way to gain weight and had already become ill several times. We were, of course, genuinely concerned about how the baby would develop as so many of the other children who lived at the landfill had shown clear signs of stunting and malnutrition when we met them for the first time.

We sent our medic out to the settlement to check on baby Pete, and we learned that his mom was not producing enough breast milk for his survival. She told us that it was difficult to feed Pete because her clothes were so contaminated with the garbage she dug through each day. There was no easy way for her to even wash. She had tried to nurse her baby the best she could, but soon after he would begin vomiting or develop diarrhea, both dangerous conditions in any small newborn.

While we always encourage breastfeeding, after discussing the situation with Pete's mom, we quickly arranged for some essential baby supplies, including high quality formula and bottled water, to be delivered so he could safely feed. We visited Pete regularly, closely tracking his height and weight each month to make sure he made progress physically. By the time he began taking his first steps, it was clear he was developing into a strong and energetic little boy who was very curious about his difficult surroundings.

As soon as Pete turned 3, his mom gave permission for him to climb aboard the LWB tuk-tuk and head to his first day of preschool, which he absolutely loves. He adores the playground, the toys, and writing his letters on the whiteboard. He also made a wonderful set of new friends who enjoy his outgoing personality. Pete's mom shared with us that each day when he returns to the landfill, he can't wait to tell her everything he did in class. There is now so much excitement in their home with all the new experiences this wonderful little boy gets to have at school. With a shy smile, she told our team, "I feel so proud of my son."

Pete's future has taken a different path now with ready access to learning. He is so clever and curious that I have no doubt he'll do well in his studies with LWB's continued support. By getting such an early start at good nutrition and education, Pete now has a real chance to someday leave the landfill behind.

I once read a statistic that over 700 million people around the world have never learned to read; sadly, a majority of that illiteracy rate is tied to being poor. According to one study I read by the UN, if all children in low-income countries were taught even the most basic reading skills, it is estimated that over 170 million people could escape severe poverty. From simply learning to read.

When I think about our work with the children at the landfill and see how students like Mercy and Pete thrive when given a chance to go to school, I know our world often misses out on its most precious resource…all the possibilities inside the human mind. How many Thomas Edisons or George Washington Carvers will never get their chance to help change the world for the better because right at this moment they are picking through waste and broken glass to afford their next meal?

So much of what we become hinges on whether there are people who believe in us. Sadly, many children begin to feel that they have no right to even dream after being judged and looked down upon because of their circumstances. What an enormous loss. Instead of focusing on the differences we outwardly see amongst each other, we should seek the commonalities. We must purposely strive for even deeper compassion and, yes, that little bit of awe as well.

Every few years our board of directors discusses once again our charity's mission statement since it is so important for any organization to stay true to its mission. Our mission statement has changed over the years, as we moved from providing care solely to orphaned children in China to now helping vulnerable children in many countries. Our vision statement, on the other hand, has never wavered, because it came to me one day through prayer:

> *LWB's vision is to provide the most loving and compassionate help possible to orphaned and impoverished children, and to show the world that every child, regardless of his or her needs, deserves to experience love and be treated with dignity and care.*

I hold as an essential truth that every child born, no matter their location, deserves to feel they are valued. Every child, regardless of status, deserves dignity, healthcare, and education. We can never stop reaching for that goal, no matter the challenges. For when given the opportunity to show the promise held inside them, every child can contribute their own unique gifts to the world.

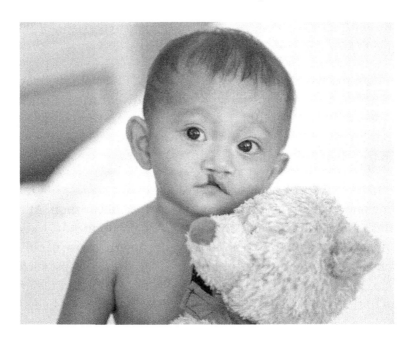

Chapter 7: Flexibility

Life is not a straight line. We should walk with courage and hope that God has a beautiful purpose for all expected and unexpected events.

Sarah Karungi, LWB-Uganda Medical Nurse Manager

Ask my children whether or not their mom was a planner when they were little, and they will probably start laughing. I took my lessons as a Girl Scout seriously. We didn't head off on any vacation as a family without me basically mapping out the entire destination months in advance. I'd research all the mom-and-pop restaurants we'd visit, the back road attractions along the way (organized by highway exit), and exactly how many outfits and extra pairs of shoes were needed for any possible weather condition.

I am thankful that with age, and a lot of international travel, I've learned that some of the most wonderful adventures we get to experience in life unfold without rigid planning. And sometimes, even when our best laid plans go completely awry, the memories we make are remarkably more meaningful.

In 2015, I spent most of July visiting our programs in China, spending one week in the southwestern province of Guizhou. At the time, this province was one of China's poorest economically, but one of the richest when it came to natural beauty and diversity of culture. Guizhou is home to many of China's ethnic minority groups, such as the Miao, Yi, Dong, and Bai peoples. The year before, I had the good fortune to stay in the home of a local Miao family in Upper Langde village, an experience I will treasure for the rest of my life. I remember walking through the rice fields early in the morning, as the sun was coming up through the mist on the mountains, and coming upon one of the village's intricate, hand-carved wooden bridges. All I could think was, "This is something like out of a dream."

At that time, we had been helping orphaned children in Guizhou for over a decade but had only recently begun doing projects for extremely rural villages which were home to many of China's "Left Behind" kids. It is estimated that more than 60 million children in China grow up without the care of their parents, left behind when their moms and dads headed to the larger cities to find work. Many of these children are being raised by elderly and often ill grandparents, while others must fend for themselves completely.

On this summer trip, I traveled with my teenage daughter Anna, who had been adopted from China as a baby, and LWB's director from Beijing, Cindy Wu. We were traveling to some of the most remote regions of Guizhou Province, not usually on many tourists' itineraries at the time due to the often-dangerous road conditions. I was grateful to be given this opportunity, and I was also very appreciative of our amazing driver, Mr. Guang. He navigated streams, rockslides, and winding roads which would suddenly just end in an enormous dirt pile on the side of the mountain. He took the term "four-wheeling" to a whole new level for us. As we drove through the province, the thought that kept coming to my mind was that humans might have been trying their best to "tame the mountain," but the landslides, boulders, and raging rivers still seemed to be winning instead.

Anna and I were in the back seat of the van, laughing hysterically as the jagged and uneven dirt roads would cause us to suddenly fly out of our seats into one another. Mr. Guang was a man on a mission, determined to make up speed and get us to the first village on our detailed travel plan while we still had daylight. Suddenly, he turned a sharp bend in the road and came upon a massive fallen fir tree completely blocking the path. We all hopped out to see if the giant timber could be pushed out of the way, but, of course, it was futile. Nature had won again. Mr. Guang had no choice but to back up the long dirt road until we found another turn we could take. When asked if he knew where the narrow path would lead us, he shrugged his shoulders and said, "I guess we'll soon find out."

After about an hour of driving through the mountains, the road began to head downward. We could see a small river village up ahead, filled with traditional wooden stilt houses and a tall, wooden drum tower. We knew then that we were heading to a Dong village, as their unique drum towers represent the very spirit of their community. These beautiful wooden structures serve as the village's most important meeting place, holding festivals and bringing people together both physically and spiritually.

The Dong people are honored for their choral singing, which has been declared a world treasure by the UN. In fact, the Dong didn't even have a written language until one was created for them in the 1950s, as they preferred to keep their history in stories and songs. Singing is an essential part of Dong culture. Their courtship rituals involve teenagers getting together to sing love songs in groups before breaking off to sing individually to each other. If the chemistry is right, a match will be made.

I had been blessed to hear a professional Dong choral performance in the capital city of Guiyang the year before, and the haunting sound of their voices had given me chills. Before we had begun our trip this time, I shared with our director Cindy that I was praying we could hear more singing in the local villages we visited, but she explained that the songs are mostly for ceremonies and festivals. She was sure that the villages would be very quiet since many young people have moved away to find work.

Our van soon pulled into what we learned was Biapa Dong Village. It appeared to be almost empty, and no one was near the large drum tower in the center of the community. Suddenly, however, we heard the unmistakable sound of Dong singing, and I grabbed Cindy's arm in excitement. We quickly hurried through the narrow alleyways to see if we could find the source. The village had no electricity the day we were there; all we could see was a dark doorway of a small wooden house. But the music coming from that entrance was incredible. We inched closer to listen, not wanting to intrude, but then a grandma sitting quietly on the stoop out front motioned us to go inside.

Inside the small room sat about a dozen Dong teenage boys, who told us they were practicing their love songs because the very next weekend they were going to a neighboring village with the hope of finding girlfriends. When asked, "At what age do most get married in this village," they replied, "Just as soon as you can find a girl." One outgoing teen explained that in the Dong culture, boys become men on their 15th birthday, allowing them to shoulder a family's responsibility. He smiled and said that's why the younger you can get married the better, and the rest of the teens all agreed. They invited us to pull up a wooden stool to sit and listen, and for the next hour we sat spellbound.

Hanging all around the simple room were the village pipas, a four-stringed instrument that has been played in China for over 2,000 years. We were honored when they took down their oldest ceremonial one to be used in a song for us. The day got even more surreal when my 16-year-old daughter Anna, who has a beautiful voice herself, was finally convinced by the youth to sing an American love song in return.

For the next few moments, I had to keep pinching myself to see if I was really sitting in a hidden mountain valley listening to my daughter sing "A Thousand Years" to teenage boys in a remote Dong village. Life certainly can be filled with the most unexpected surprises, can't it?

The hospitality we were shown that day was immense, and I wondered how many of us would welcome complete strangers into our homes if we saw them wandering around aimlessly in our neighborhood. When our stomachs began to growl, we asked the grandma if there was a village restaurant where we could get a meal before we headed on our way. After shaking her head that nothing like that existed in the small village, she quickly made up some delicious homemade noodles for us despite our protests. We left as new friends, promising to send warm clothing and school supplies for the children as soon as possible.

As Mr. Guang slowly wound our van up the mountain to find a major roadway, I gave thanks that our detailed travel itinerary had gone completely off target. Thanks to the giant fir tree that had fallen and blocked our path, something even more extraordinary had been revealed. It was a great reminder that being willing to adjust when life throws unexpected things our way is definitely something to strive for...although I did wonder that night if my young daughter was inadvertently now engaged, by answering back to the boys' sweet love songs with one of her own.

When you look at your own life, where do you think you fall on the flexibility scale? Do you adapt easily to change, or does your blood pressure have a tendency to inevitably rise? COVID certainly brought the concept of flexibility to the forefront of 2020. Even those who always want to firmly control every detail of their lives found themselves having to adapt significantly. Friends and families, who could no longer see each other in person for safety reasons, had to think of new ways to feel connected. Anxious brides and grooms, planning big in-person celebrations, had to send virtual invitations and video links instead. Many of our wonderful LWB volunteers are teachers, who suddenly found themselves switching to online learning. I hung up the phone one day in amazement after speaking with our IT volunteer Nancy Williams, who is a teacher in Ohio. She told me that a large number of her students didn't have access to computers or the Internet. She was teaching virtually all day to those who did and then assembling packets of hardcopy lessons that she'd drive around delivering to the other kids at night. COVID made our entire world have to rethink and regroup, as all our carefully laid plans were toppled by a virus which spread at the speed of light.

The international work of Love Without Boundaries was of course impacted in many ways as well. One of our favorite projects over the years has always been our annual cleft surgery trips. We sent our first medical team overseas back in 2004, to provide surgery for 50 orphaned children who had been born with cleft lip and palate. Every year since, we assembled doctors, nurses, and volunteers from different countries for a special week of healing that our community had always rallied behind.

The trips served several purposes: first, of course, to change the lives of children through high-quality operations. But there were other essential goals as well. In many countries around the world, superstitions still abound surrounding children born with medical needs. In some parts of Africa for example, it is thought that children born with birth defects are a result of sorcery. In Cambodia, a country where many believe strongly in reincarnation, some believe birth defects are a punishment for something the baby did in a previous life. We always looked forward to our LWB medical trips, as they were wonderful opportunities to provide education in a local community. Having accurate medical knowledge about special needs is one of the best ways to overcome superstition and fear.

On our 2018 cleft trip to Gansu, China, for example, the LWB team worked hard to dispel common myths surrounding cleft lip. One of the young patients we met was a little boy named Adan. His family were from the Hui minority and lived on the Tibetan plateau. They had traveled a very long distance to see our surgeons. Adan's father told us how much he struggled to make ends meet by picking up junk and trash to sell. Before their son was born, he worked in a plastics factory, but one day he had an accident on the job and lost several fingers on his right hand. Things became even more difficult for the family when he was then diagnosed with TB. When their son Adan was born with cleft lip, they felt the sun had fallen out of the sky and could not understand why misfortune continued to rain down on their family.

Adan's family loved their little boy, however, and so they never quit searching for a way to get him the medical care he needed. They once had an opportunity for Adan to have surgery in Beijing, but they were unable to come up with the money to pay for their travel there. Adan's mom said it was probably for the best, as she was afraid she'd get lost in such a big city since she wouldn't be able to read the words on any of the signs.

We were so happy that this rural family had learned about our visiting team, especially when Adan's mom explained that people in their remote region sincerely believe that cleft is a curse. Children born with this condition often are not allowed to go outside. Many families will not even seek medical help, as they are told that a birth defect only occurs if the parents or grandparents did bad things. To save the reputation of the family, a child born with cleft is usually either abandoned or hidden away. Our local facilitator carefully explained to Adan's parents that cleft happens all over the world, with a high percentage of cases happening in Asia. Adan's lip had nothing to do with being cursed; the tissue simply hadn't closed properly during pregnancy.

Dr. Chris Tolan, one of the wonderful surgeons on that trip, reassured the parents that he would take good care of their son and give baby Adan a truly beautiful cleft repair. The smile on Adan's mother's face following surgery was wonderful to see. She said she couldn't wait to take her little boy back home to their village, because she knew his future had been forever changed that day by the LWB team.

On our cleft trip to Cambodia in 2017, similar stories were shared. A few months earlier, we had met an adorable baby girl named Avery, who lived with her family in a small village near the Thai border. Her mother told us that when she learned the baby had cleft, she cried for days because of all the superstitions surrounding this special need. When Avery first arrived into the world, the family was told that their tiny daughter should be given to the monks to raise, as it would be the only way the little girl could atone for the terrible mistakes she had obviously made in a past life. Thankfully, before the family surrendered their baby to the temple, one of our medical team members in the region met Avery's mom and explained that her cleft lip was completely correctable.

Dr. Travis Tollefson, from UC-Davis in California, had traveled with LWB to Cambodia to perform surgeries in Phnom Penh. He carefully repaired baby Avery's cleft lip before handing her to the waiting post-op nurses. It was a very touching moment when Avery's mom saw her daughter for the first time after her surgery was complete. Many parents have told us over the years that it's actually quite bittersweet to hold your baby following a cleft lip operation. A complex set of emotions washes over you. There is a feeling of joy knowing their new smile will allow an easier and brighter future, but also a deep sense of loss that you'll never again see the face you first fell in love with.

Planning a successful overseas medical exchange takes almost a year of logistics. The schedules of doctors and nurses on both sides of the ocean must be coordinated, and the partner hospital needs time as well to block off an entire patient ward. After looking at several locations, we had decided that our 2020 cleft trip was going to be held in India during the month of April. Our team would be traveling to the far northern region of Assam to work in partnership with Mission Smile, a domestic charity dedicated to helping children with cleft. Airline tickets were purchased, international medical licenses were issued, and mounds of needed supplies were gathered. We couldn't wait for spring to arrive. Unfortunately, COVID arrived faster. In mid-March, as most of the world began sheltering in place, we made the difficult decision to call off the 2020 cleft trip. For the first time in

LWB history, the special "week of healing" to help children receive surgery would not be able to take place.

While COVID had canceled one of our favorite projects completely, I knew it wasn't going to stop our community's desire to help kids receive the medical care they needed. I was soon to find out that by having the pandemic "topple fir trees" to block international travel, our eyes were opened to a new opportunity that we might have missed before.

When I wrote earlier about the remarkable story of Grace, the beautiful girl whose abdomen had filled with countless tumors, I mentioned that a doctor in Uganda, Dr. Martin Situma, helped us get the testing and medical permissions needed to send her to Belgium for treatment. Dr. Situma practices in Mbarara, Uganda, and he is highly respected in the world of pediatric surgery. He knew he wanted to become a physician when he was still in high school, working extremely hard at his studies to earn a position for medical school at Makerere University in Kampala. Following his internship, he worked deep upcountry, where the medical needs were great and where he discovered his hands had a gift to perform surgery. He also realized that his heart was drawn toward helping children, but at the time there was no available training in Uganda for pediatric surgery.

Thankfully, in 2010, he was offered an opportunity to go to South Africa for a two-year pediatric surgery fellowship at the University of Cape Town. He excelled in that program and was then offered a spot to receive additional training in Kenya, soon earning board certification in this very specialized field. Dr. Situma is now the Chief of Pediatric Surgery at both Mbarara Regional Referral Hospital and at Holy Innocents Children's Hospital.

It is incredible to think that in Uganda, with a population of over 22 million children, only six pediatric surgeons were in practice in 2020. Dr. Situma is on the forefront of helping to train the next generation. He continually searches for new ways to help even more Ugandan children, especially those whose poverty keeps them from the medical care they desperately need. His deep faith is what gives him the strength to keep persevering.

Soon after our cleft trip to India was abruptly canceled, I received an email from Dr. Situma. He asked if LWB would like to partner with him and Holy Innocents Hospital on a one-week surgical camp to heal 50 children whose families could not afford their operations. He wanted to gather surgeons from across the country to help alleviate the children's suffering. I read "one week, 50 patients," and my heart did a somersault. It was time for LWB to adapt our international medical trip model to a 100% domestic one instead.

Instead of patients with cleft, the mission planned by Dr. Situma was going to be primarily for children with inguinal hernias. We all probably know someone who has suffered from this condition, when muscle tissue in the groin or lower abdomen is weak or damaged. Tissue, sometimes including the intestines, is then able to break through and bulge outwards – often causing immense pain. Inguinal hernias are one of the most common surgery needs in children, affecting 1 to 5% of all children born. On this trip, many of the children who would be coming to see the surgeons sadly had been living in agony for years.

As we began discussing the logistics of holding a week-long surgery mission, we worked together to finalize the budget. The cost of medical care in Uganda seems extremely low to most people living in Europe or America. A child's hernia repair in most regions of Uganda can usually be done at a private hospital for under $300. For families living in extreme poverty, however, trying to feed their children on just pennies a day, $300 might as well be a million. Holy Innocents had agreed to reduce their medical costs even further for this special week, which would allow us to support a child's complete surgery for a $100 fee.

One thing that my friends in Uganda have taught me over the years is that when making plans to provide help in a community, it is always a good idea to prepare for extras. It is well given advice as the weeks leading up to the mission clearly showed. As news of the free surgical camp spread throughout the region, Dr. Situma let us know that the numbers of waiting children continued to grow. There were now 100 children on the surgery waiting list that he was hoping could be healed. His team was willing to operate from morning to night to make sure they all got a chance.

I was overjoyed when the LWB community stepped forward in just under a week to cover all 100 surgeries. Dr. Situma sent a special message back: "I would like the donors to know that for each amount they give, they are changing the destiny of a child for the better. May God bless them. Nothing is too small or too big when given with a willing heart."

On the first morning of the mission, before the sun even rose in the sky, the LWB team made their way to Holy Innocents Children's Hospital, located in a district known as the "land of milk and honey." Many tourists to Uganda travel through Mbarara on their way to gorilla treks, but few might realize that this town, known for agriculture and raising long-horned cattle, has now become the fastest growing region in the country.

Holy Innocents was founded in 2009 as one of the first pediatric hospitals in the country, and in January of 2019, their surgery center was completed. The importance of this cannot be overstated as many operating rooms around the world have equipment that is solely for adults, but Holy Innocents has supplies and equipment that have been specifically made and sized for the littlest patients. The hospital had set aside 40 of their 100 beds for this special mission, as well as three operating room tables.

While the doctors were preparing the surgical instruments and post-op plans for the week, the LWB team was preparing child care packs to make the children's stay at the hospital as comfortable as possible. Each care pack given by our supporters included a warm blanket, mosquito net, and of course a fun toy, along with a t-shirt stating, "Every Child Counts." As our team worked together to assemble each special package, the little patients and their families began to arrive in the now pouring rain. Many families had traveled such a long way with the hope their children would be selected for surgery. Our Ugandan director, Ronald, told us that many parents were anxious and worried, not honestly believing their children would receive free surgery, as they had already waited years for their pain to finally end. As he assured them that the medical care costs would indeed be covered by LWB, smiles and laughter broke out in the hospital courtyard. Mothers exclaimed that their prayers had finally been answered since their children had suffered for an exceptionally long time.

It was difficult to hear many of their stories. Eight-year-old Clever was so miserable with his hernia that his face was contorted in agony. His mother was a rural farmer with extremely limited funds, so when her son was first diagnosed, she was unable to afford the surgery he needed. In an attempt to relieve his constant pain, she could only offer him some hand-picked herbs, feeling enormous emotional distress to see Clever hurting for so long. Eleven-year-old Shirah's parents were farmers as well, and they told our team that she began having pain right after she was born. Shirah had waited ELEVEN YEARS to finally receive her hernia operation, and her mother was so happy that her daughter's torment would finally be relieved. Then there was 5-year-old Frank, whose mother had died when he was a tiny baby. After his father then abandoned the family, Frank and his siblings were taken in by their elderly grandmother. When he was 6 months old, Frank's grandma found out that he was suffering from a painful hernia and immediately sought medical help. Because of her great poverty, however, each time she took him to the local hospital, they would tell her to leave and return home.

As children continued to stream into the Holy Innocents compound that weekend, we soon realized there were far more than 100 hoping to be healed. At the end of the first surgery day alone, Dr. Situma and his team had performed 30 operations. Joy, one of the LWB Uganda directors, shared, "Mothers that had given up, conditions that had lasted for years, but at the end of the day, you could see smiles and hearts filled with hope once again. The mothers shared that it had been a really painful season for them, but praise be to God that this opportunity came, and the children received the healing they deserved."

The second day of the mission saw 35 little patients head into the OR. The medical team operated for 12 straight hours and added a fourth operating room table to make sure every possible child who came would receive surgery. Eight-year-old Winfred, who lost her birth mom at around 3 weeks of age, was one of the children on the surgical list that day. When Winfred was 2 years old, she started experiencing pain in her abdomen. Her new stepmother was accused by their village of practicing witchcraft on the child. To prove her innocence, the stepmom took Winfred to see a doctor for testing, and it was discovered that the little girl had a hernia. Unfortunately, Winfred's family did not have the funds needed for an operation, so she had waited four additional years for an end to her agony.

Another child operated on that day was Baby Maria. Her mother had been in true distress since her birth as Maria had been unable to keep any milk in her stomach. Each time she breastfed, Maria would violently throw up. The baby was born weighing five pounds, but Maria's weight soon dropped to just four. She quickly became listless. Her mom took her to a local hospital where she was diagnosed with pyloric stenosis, a condition where the muscles in the stomach block food from entering the small intestine. Without surgery, life-threatening dehydration and electrolyte imbalance set in.

Unfortunately, the first hospital Baby Maria was taken to said that nothing could be done and sent her home without treatment. When Maria's mom saw her little girl getting increasingly sick, she rushed her to a regional hospital seeking help, and they finally agreed to operate. Just as they were planning to take the baby back for surgery, however, the hospital lost power. Thankfully, the doctors at that facility called Dr. Situma, and Maria was transferred immediately to Holy Innocents as an emergency case. We were thankful the OR was already prepped and ready to save her beautiful life.

On the third day of the mission, the doctors surpassed 100 surgeries, with the courtyard of the hospital still filling with anxious families. One of the children who arrived was a beautiful little girl named Lucia. Lucia's mother told us that when Lucia was just a toddler, her eyes "got so sick." Lucia's mom didn't know what the actual condition was, but the doctor they visited said her little girl needed immediate medical intervention. Tragically, because of the impoverished family's inability to pay, the spreading infection went unchecked. When Lucia was 3 years old, the doctor felt nothing more could be done except to remove the little girl's eyes.

A few months after Lucia became blind, her abdomen began to swell in a startling way. When her mom took her to the hospital, she was told that her daughter had a large umbilical hernia that needed immediate surgery. An umbilical hernia occurs when part of the bowel or fatty tissue in the abdomen pokes through a weak spot near the belly button. Lucia's case was an extreme one, with the bulge in her abdomen now larger than a grapefruit. As a poor farmer, however, Lucia's mom couldn't come up with the funds needed for the operation her daughter needed.

We were so thankful we could help Lucia finally get the hernia repair she needed. Her mom shared that the burden of not being able to provide for her daughter medically had been a heavy one, but now she felt only joy in her heart. She asked us to send a message to the kind donors who made Lucia's operation possible, telling us that, while she was poor in material goods, her faith was abundant. She had asked God to bless each person who had brought relief to her little girl. The next morning on the hospital ward, our team couldn't hold back their tears when little Lucia stood up and sweetly sang a song of thanksgiving.

Usually, the final day of a medical mission is scheduled to be slower, as the team winds down a week that is almost always physically exhausting. That was not the case for this first surgery camp in Mbarara, as the surgeons continued to operate long into the night on the closing day. The doctors and nurses were determined to help as many children as possible receive surgery, bringing the total number of operations completed in just five days to a staggering 187.

This special week at Holy Innocents was such a wonderful illustration of why the Ugandan people are celebrated for their spirit of generosity. Did you know that the small country of Uganda accepts more people fleeing persecution and war-torn lands than any other country on earth? Over 1.4 million refugees have found safety in her borders. When asked why such a poverty-stricken country would continue to help others in need, many Ugandans simply answer, "Because it's the right thing to do." Just like Lucia's mom, those who have nothing material to give still offer their generous prayers.

During this surgery week in Uganda, we saw kindness overflowing. Originally, four doctors had agreed to see patients. As fliers were posted and news spread on the radio, however, medical professionals from around the country began making the journey to help and to serve. From the far north down to the south, 25 nurses and 11 doctors arrived at the surgery mission to offer their time. What a gift they provided. By the final day, over 300 families had come that week with a humble request for their children to receive medical care. That meant over 120 more children were still in need of essential surgery. It was time to roll up our sleeves again and dream even bigger.

Whenever I think of the disappointment we felt originally after our surgery trip to India had to be canceled, I switch my mind to this special week at Holy Innocents instead. I remind myself that the beautiful thing about endings is that they can usher in new beginnings as well. While our international cleft trips had to be postponed during COVID, the partnerships we built on this first surgical camp in Uganda were the start of many more children finally getting the medical help they need.

On Christmas Day 2019, I won the award for the worst Mrs. Claus ever, tripping in my garage while carrying some wrapped presents to the car. I heard my leg snap even before I felt the reality of what I'd just done. As I attempted to army crawl across the floor to let my kids know our holiday dinner might be a wee bit late, I was thinking it sure would have been nice if my tibia could have done me the favor of being a little more flexible. X-rays showed my leg was far from the definition of that word though, and over the next two months, my rigid walking boot never became my friend. I would sigh a bit each time I reached for my crutches, wishing that our bones had the magic ability to bend without breaking.

I'm going to use my broken leg memory to raise the question of when we should be unyielding as we go about our lives and when we should choose to bend or switch paths. You might have heard a quote frequently attributed to Thomas Jefferson that says, *"In matters of style, swim with the current; in matters of principle, stand like a rock."* It's a nice quote, overlaid on several beautiful Instagram images, even though every source checked (including Mr. Jefferson's own papers), don't show him as ever really saying it. But obviously since the anonymous quote has been floating around out there for over a hundred years, it shows that the question of whether to hold firm or change tactics is one as old as time.

We have certainly had to decide at LWB which answer we were comfortable with over the years, working with government officials who often want things done their way alone. When do we completely walk away if something isn't in line with our project models and when do we adapt to make sure children receive care? We had to ask ourselves those very questions with our foster care program in China.

As I have already mentioned, our charity had a vibrant and highly successful foster care program which began in 2004. We moved thousands of children out of institutional care over the years, in cities from the far west of China down to the deep south. The children's transformations were not only life-changing, but often life-saving. I can't begin to describe the number of babies, weak and failing to thrive after having their bottles propped in orphanage cribs, who then regained their health after having a caring foster mom hand feed them.

Finding foster parents in China had never been difficult for us, since the majority of families had lived under the One Child policy. In many of the regions where we worked, we would have families lining up to apply as a foster parent, especially once their only biological child had grown up and moved on. We were blessed with some truly amazing families, as our criteria didn't involve how wealthy they were but instead how devoted and kind. In fact, most of our foster parents lived in very meager surroundings.

In Qiandongnan, for example, which was once considered a very rural part of Guizhou Province, most of our foster moms lived in very humble homes, with stone floors and a small stove in the center of the room. The babies would be bundled up in padded coats and then tied to their mama's backs in beautiful, hand-embroidered baby carriers. While their lodgings might not have been grand, the care and concern they showed their foster children was priceless. It was always a true joy to see a thin baby who had entered orphanage care become the very picture of health after being moved into a local home.

I had many conversations with officials throughout the country, however, who felt that using rural families was a disservice to the children. As China continued to build larger and more expensive orphanages in even the most remote locations, the opinion that children would be best served by living inside the fancier facilities began to grow and take hold. One by one, from 2016 to 2018, our foster care programs began to be closed. In many locations, the children were given less than a day's notice before having to say goodbye to the families they had often been with for years. We were devastated. Although the children were moved back to multi-million-dollar facilities, you will never convince me that children should be raised in institutions. Remember my question above about what things in your life you refuse to bend on? Institutional care was one of mine. No one could ever convince me that orphanages trumped families, despite having a lot of people who've tried.

One of the things in our work which upsets us deeply is when an orphaned child is in a GOOD placement and then are forced to relocate. All of us at LWB continually think about the attachment cycle, as we want every child to feel safe and secure. Each time a child is moved, we recognize that their ability to trust again can be harmed. I've seen firsthand, far too many times, the enormous trauma and grief that arises when a child's family (foster or biological) disappears in an instant. It's why with every new case we accept, we begin discussing permanency. For without what many in the adoption world call a "forever home," a child's placement can come crashing down in an instant at the whim of a new official.

If you will humor me for a moment while I go into "company speak," here is the official child-centered pathway we've implemented at LWB:

1. Empower the local community to identify children at risk of abandonment, abuse, and neglect, and provide support to strengthen family bonds when possible

2. Search for birth parents separated from children through relinquishment or abandonment, and plan for safe and healthy reunifications

3. Create kinship care plans with extended family members when children cannot be reunited with birth parents

4. Strengthen local foster care systems and encourage domestic adoption for children who are unable to live with biological families

5. Advocate for permanency through international adoption when a domestic placement is improbable

In a nutshell, we want children to stay with their biological parents first and foremost. In the sad event that can't happen, we hope relatives can care for the child. If that's not possible, then we want foster care over orphanages, with the goal of domestic adoption. And if all of the above is still a "no" for permanency, we advocate for an international adoption placement, if allowed. Every child deserves a family.

Over the last decade, I have loved seeing the rise of legal, domestic adoptions in China. Now, whenever we take in a child who was found abandoned as a preemie for example, I know that they will graduate from our healing homes straight to domestic adoption. But in a country where 98% of children entering orphanage care have some sort of medical need, there are still a lot of special needs that keep abandoned children from being chosen in their country of birth. Visible special needs, such as albinism or a missing limb, are still exceedingly difficult for domestic placement. Severe heart issues or conditions such as cerebral palsy are also medical needs which will make a domestic adoption almost impossible. And, today in 2021, cognitive issues almost always sentence an orphaned child to a life in institutional care.

I know that the majority of stories I like to share about our work are those with happy endings. A heart is healed, a degree is earned, or an orphaned child is chosen by a family. We all love those stories, because we want the absolute best for each child who comes into our hands. The reality though, is that a lot of our work involves deep sadness. Sick children pass away. Far too many are abandoned. And many orphaned children, who so deserve permanency and a caring family of their very own, spend a life in institutional care instead.

One of the children whom I wished greatly to have a better life is a boy named Cory. I met him for the first time when he was just a baby. He had been born with bilateral clubfeet, a birth defect which caused his feet to turn in completely. Clubfoot is considered a very correctable medical need, with most children undergoing either casting or surgery to straighten the foot's position. We first got involved with Cory as part of our nutrition program at his orphanage. At age one, we moved him to a foster home and arranged for him to get the medical care he needed to be able to walk and run. He was a beautiful, curious little boy, and his special need was one that usually was chosen by families quickly. For years, however, the orphanage did not complete his adoption file, so he missed out on being chosen as a younger child, which the majority of adoptive families still prefer.

Cory absolutely thrived with his foster family, however. We could tell he had one of those minds which loved trying to figure things out. Whenever we would visit his home, we'd bring toys like Legos and model kits. Before we even had unfolded the instructions, Cory would be trying to piece them together. He was extremely close to his foster dad, and he loved helping his father work on their motorbike, handing him tools and trying to figure out how everything on the engine was put together. He would also go jogging in the mornings with his foster dad and delighted in playing soccer with the other children in the neighborhood.

One of the things that touched our hearts the most about Cory is that he was also an excellent foster brother to every child we placed in his family. When we would bring treats or toys to his home, he always made sure everyone else had theirs first, before agreeing to take one of his own. There was an innate kindness within Cory that endeared him to everyone he met. I knew when he was younger, it was difficult for him to watch each of his foster siblings go on to be chosen by adoptive families. He had to ask himself when it would be his turn.

As Cory grew to school age, we arranged for him to begin attending a private kindergarten near his foster home. It was then that we began to get the first reports that Cory struggled with traditional school…not from a social or emotional aspect; he quickly made lots of friends, and the teachers would always report how kind and polite he was. He won many red ribbons for his positive attitude and being a classroom helper. Learning to read, however, became a major struggle, and the often-strict Chinese methods of teaching were very difficult for a child with an undiagnosed learning disability.

My heart hurt when I learned Cory had trouble with his academic lessons, particularly because my youngest son from China had struggled at school as well. After many years of testing, my son TJ had been formally diagnosed with severe dyslexia. From the time he was a preschooler, I knew something was up, as learning the letters of the alphabet was an enormous battle for him. He could remember in detail every dinosaur name or fact I would read to him and could put together 500-piece Lego sets without ever looking at the directions. But if asked to read the letters C-A-T... it simply didn't compute. I vividly remember sitting in school meetings with administrators, who didn't fully know my child, trying to convince me that I should consider full-time special education for my son.

What I knew as TJ's mom, however, was that he is very clever and insightful. His brain just didn't want to learn to read in the same way as others. One of my favorite TJ stories that illustrates his quick wit was when he made the decision to not wear a prosthetic for his arm amputation. He had explained that since he'd been born with a missing limb, the heavy prosthetic he'd been fitted with never felt right. It was bulky, and he felt he could do everything he wanted with one hand just fine. When we went to our final prosthetic appointment, to let them know his decision, the exasperated technician said, "TJ, I want you to imagine yourself on a fancy date someday, trying to impress a girl. Do you really want to have to ask her to cut up your steak because you won't wear a prosthetic?" Without missing a beat, TJ quipped back, "I'll just order the pasta." Touché.

This was the same engagement and common sense I had seen Cory display as well over the years, when he would joke and laugh with his foster parents and neighbors. I kept hoping that someday, through adoption, he'd be able to get the extra intervention services he needed, just like my son TJ had. With the right support, my son ended up loving school. I wanted the same opportunity for Cory.

We had no way to do formal diagnostic testing when Cory was in our care, however, so we weren't able to know if he had a processing disorder like dyslexia or one of the many other learning disabilities which impact millions of school-aged children in the US alone. But I knew that without a permanent family, who would advocate for him to receive all possible education support, his future would be extremely uncertain. When the school near Cory's home said he could no longer attend since he couldn't master reading, we knew that Cory needed a way out of the institutional system more than ever.

Thankfully, his orphanage had finally agreed to file his adoption paperwork, and I was absolutely confident that Cory would find a home since his special need of clubfeet had already been treated. I waited for the great news that a family had stepped forward, but it didn't come. I then watched as his adoption file made the rounds at multiple agencies without a family committing to bring him home. I couldn't understand it. I had watched Cory grow from a baby to a curious preschooler to a truly kind and polite little boy. Why wasn't anyone stepping forward to bring him home?

When Cory turned 10 and still hadn't been chosen for adoption, I made a special trip to visit him at his foster home. He was still the kind and cheerful boy I remembered from previous visits. He helped us carry the snacks we'd brought into his home, and immediately asked if we wanted a chair to rest our feet. Just like I remembered, he instinctively offered the treats to his foster sister and parents first, before taking one for himself. I watched him laughing and talking easily with his foster dad, whom he clearly loved deeply. At the end of our visit, however, Cory's foster father took us aside quietly and told us he'd been diagnosed with a severe heart issue. He said his biggest worry was not being able to foster much longer, as he didn't want Cory to be moved back to institutional care. His dad then told me how much he wanted Cory to be adopted. He kept saying that Cory had enormous potential if he could get an education, but it simply wouldn't happen in his current situation. His dad was trying to teach Cory Chinese characters at home, but he desperately wanted Cory to go to school. He knew the only way that would happen is if he were adopted by a family who could find him the special services he needed.

When Cory walked over and heard his foster father talking about adoption, he immediately grabbed onto his hand, saying, "This is my dad; I want to stay with my dad." My heart grew heavy as I wished for Cory's sake that things could be that simple. We had employed his family as foster parents for over ten years, and they had cared for dozens of children for us during that time. As much as I knew they loved and truly cared for Cory, I also knew the father was being very honest with us when he said his failing health would not allow him to foster forever. I sadly realized yet again just how many orphaned children's lives are so completely beyond their control.

Before we left, Cory sang us a traditional Chinese song, with an embarrassed smile that any young boy would have when asked to perform for strangers. As I listened to his sweet, clear voice, I prayed that a family would want to make him their own. Just like my own son TJ, I hoped that Cory would one day get the opportunity to discover how he learns best, with a permanent family cheering him on the whole way. It weighed on my heart to think of this all-around nice kid going through the trauma of losing the foster father he loved so dearly. I knew his grief and sadness when that inevitable day arrived would either be faced with an adoptive family by his side or completely on his own, returned to the orphanage he left as a baby. I sure knew for which one of those I was praying.

This is where our work really hurts. When it comes to a topic like adoption, we can gather metrics and analyze trends and discuss what new regulations will mean for the process. The reality, though, is that all the statistics and numbers we see in reports are ACTUAL LITTLE KIDS. They are living, breathing children who depend wholly on adults to act in their best interest, and we all know that doesn't always happen. I couldn't magically give Cory a permanent family, no matter how much I wished it. With each passing month he wasn't chosen, he inched closer to the day he would no longer qualify for placement. At that time in China, that would happen on his 14th birthday.

When I arrived back to the US, I was finally given the opportunity to see Cory's actual adoption file. What I read made me want to put my head down and weep. I had been imagining an adoption file summary which said, "Cory loves building with Legos. He is cheerful and polite, and always kind to his foster sister. Cory's a huge help to his parents, responsible with chores, and respectful to seniors in his neighborhood." Instead, whoever had created Cory's adoption file said he had the intellectual capabilities of an infant. It went on to state that

Cory was a child with extreme cognitive delays who could not communicate well with others. Clearly someone at the orphanage who had not visited Cory in foster care had heard he struggled at school and had decided to label him forever on paper as being unable to learn or ever live on his own.

I could not believe this was the file that potential families were seeing. The sterile description of "Boy, severe cognitive needs" was NOT the child we had come to know over the years. It wasn't a correct portrayal of Cory, who recited poetry, built contraptions, and loved playing ball. We began advocating in an even bigger way for Cory to find his family, but still no one stepped forward.

In the summer of 2017, Cory's devoted foster father had a major heart attack. This kind man had fostered children with LWB for over a decade, and the news was difficult to hear. We were thankful that he was able to survive, but he remained extremely weak. The orphanage then moved Cory to a new foster home. While the family was very nice, Cory's grief over losing the only father he'd known and adored was immense. How do you even measure the impact that losing everyone you love has on a child's heart?

Soon after Cory moved to his new foster home, we began hearing rumors that his province was considering an end to all foster care. We increased our advocacy efforts for Cory and offered an ever-increasing adoption grant in the hope that a caring family would hear about this wonderful boy. While many people expressed interest, it only took one look at his dismally inaccurate adoption file to have them decline the placement.

In April 2018, Cory's life was again shattered when all children in home-based care in his province were called back to their institutions. Our foster care program in Cory's town, which had been running for 14 straight years, was closed overnight. Another door in Cory's hurting heart was slammed closed.

After being pulled back into the orphanage, Cory spent the next two years of his life living mainly in one single room. He helped the nannies clean and care for the children with more severe special needs. His love of building and tinkering continued. He would take the broken toys and try to piece them together to create new ones. As one of the only children in the orphanage who was mobile, he would sometimes get permission to go out to sit on the rusty, broken swing set out back. When our manager would visit and then send reports, he described Cory as a lonely boy.

As the pandemic spread in China, all the orphanages in Cory's province went into full lock-down; no one was allowed to go in or out. We were no longer able to visit Cory in person but were grateful when we learned that he had formed a good relationship with one of the nannies working there. Wanting so desperately to feel like he belonged, he spent almost every waking moment by her side.

By the end of the lock-down, Cory told the orphanage director he no longer wanted a family. He was adamant that he wanted to stay in China with his nanny instead. At the age of 12, Cory asked that his adoption file be closed. My heart sank, because I understood that after losing his foster parents, and then being pulled back into the orphanage, what Cory really wanted was the ability to feel control of his life. We all knew his heart had been broken, and so I was grateful that this new nanny had made him feel safe again. But a paid nanny is not a mother, and I knew far too well that everything about orphanage life, including the staffing, is unstable. I continued to pray that he would change his mind and keep open the option of having a permanent family someday.

In September 2020, Cory's world collapsed all over again. The decision was made to close his orphanage, since all of the children living there except him had very complex special needs. The children would be moved to a much larger facility in a bigger city, where LWB did not have any contacts. Cory sobbed as they took him away from the nanny he had come to love. This time, he was moved beyond our ability to offer support during the transition.

We learned a few weeks later that the decision was made at the new orphanage to close Cory's adoption file for good. This incredibly kind boy, who would have blessed a family in so many remarkable ways, had lost the chance to escape the institutional system. It still hurts to look at his photos. I hope his new caregivers have learned of Cory's mechanical talent. Perhaps he will someday be able to work at the orphanage as a maintenance person. I pray he will feel loved.

Cory is why permanency for orphaned children, at the earliest age possible, must always be a primary goal. Every child needs a lasting, legal family to be his or her advocate in life. If Cory would have had parents step forward when he was younger, they could have helped him navigate the world of learning disabilities. They would have been his biggest cheerleaders in helping him find a place in the world where he could thrive. While government officials and adoption policies can change frequently, the love of a devoted family endures. It's a love which can move mountains, and the love every child deserves. I am heartbroken that a permanent family is something Cory will now never know.

I share the story of Cory, not only because I care deeply about him but also because watching our foster programs close showed us there are times that we must be flexible in how our charity work is done. Up until the time foster homes began shuttering in China, I had been absolutely unbending in my insistence that LWB would only do foster care in local communities. An increasing number of orphanages over the years had begun building small apartments inside their new facilities so that children could remain on the orphanage grounds but live in a more family-like setting. We had been asked frequently to consider such an arrangement, but the older children I knew who lived in some of those facilities had told me it wasn't the same as growing up in a typical neighborhood.

There had always been something really wonderful to me about how we could move children beyond the locked gates of an orphanage compound into a real community. We loved seeing a child be able to go to the market with mom, dance in the park with grandma, or ride scooters with friends in the neighborhood. We loved knowing that giving neighbors the ability to meet and care about orphaned children (often for the first time in their lives) was breaking down the deep stigma surrounding those who are abandoned. Each time an orphanage would ask us to consider on-site care, we always politely declined.

What we had learned, however, in having so many children be returned to their orphanages after 2016, is that we often then lose the ability to continue being their advocates. LWB provides so much more than a foster home when a child is in our care. We believe strongly in the "whole child" model. Once a child comes into our hands, we help them reach their full potential through additional services when necessary, such as medical care or specialized nutrition. And, of course, we push like crazy to make sure they have a chance at a permanent home. We had realized that if we continued being so strict in our insistence that orphaned children should be raised in local communities, we would lose our ability to champion their worthiness.

Many years ago, I had read an article about a business strategist named Eric Ries, who had written a book for start-up entrepreneurs. One of his most quoted lines states, *"A pivot is a change in strategy without a change in vision."* Was it time for LWB to pivot in China when it came to foster care? Our vision for children living in orphanages certainly has never changed. We hold firm to the vision that every child deserves to be raised in a loving family. As orphanages across China started to ban off-site foster care, however, it was now time to sit down once again with officials. How could we bring that vital sense of family to children who now had to remain behind orphanage gates? We had to let go of our stringent requirement that children live in local neighborhoods and instead do everything we could to create families inside the institutional walls.

As of 2021, we created on-site family care programs in two Chinese orphanages. We were given wings in the facilities to renovate into small apartments, with four children per family living in each one. It wasn't easy to find foster parents willing to move inside the orphanage grounds, though, even with us providing free rent and a foster stipend. So much of life in China revolves around that sense of community that I mentioned above…walking to the local grocery, exercising with friends in the neighborhood park, having friends over for tea. So many of the orphanages now are enormous compounds, outside the bustle of the city, with no easy way to walk to a market or park offsite. Several of the first families we hired left after a month or so, as they said it was just too isolating to live inside the orphanage complex. Thankfully, however, the families we have at this moment have found a sense of community with one another. They are willing to live inside an orphanage because they've come to love their foster children.

While this program will never be quite the same as our foster care projects in other countries around the world, I have found peace in knowing that by adapting our model in China we have managed to stay connected to the children we care so dearly about. One of the little boys in our family-care program is adorable Sterling. He had first come into our hands when he was just a baby, arriving at our healing home in a malnourished state and gasping to breathe. Sterling had been born with Down syndrome, so we moved him to the heart hospital for a full evaluation since half of all babies with Down syndrome also have heart defects. We soon discovered that Sterling had a large hole between the ventricles of his heart, and the healing home nannies got to work getting him strong enough to undergo surgery.

After his heart defect was repaired, Sterling's development really began taking off. His appetite improved, and he went from sitting to crawling and then standing up. When he was moved into LWB foster care in a wonderful neighborhood, his new grandparents worked with him continually until he went from walking to a full-out run. They had a big yard behind their house, which Sterling loved to play in. He became such a fast runner that his grandparents had a hard time keeping up with him. I had to smile when in one of his early reports our manager wrote: "Every morning after getting out of bed, Sterling enjoys working with his foster grandpa out in the yard. When he first started helping, he was afraid of the family dog outside. He would initially cry whenever he would see the dog, but thankfully he's now become brave. In fact, he started chasing the dog around the yard. Now, instead of Sterling being afraid of the dog, the dog is a bit afraid of Sterling."

We definitely didn't want to lose our ability to keep helping this spirited little boy, so as rumors began to swirl that local officials would soon ban foster care, we sat down with them to discuss a new project. Thankfully, Sterling's orphanage was one of the facilities which agreed that LWB could bring family-based care onsite. We were grateful that we would be able to remain a part of Sterling's life, especially since his repaired heart would require ongoing monitoring.

Over the last few years, Sterling has continued to flourish. He remains close to his foster family and living inside the orphanage allowed him to begin attending the school that LWB had created. When his teachers noticed that he put the books he held right up to his face, we arranged for his foster mom to take him to an eye doctor for a full exam. Sterling got to choose his very own glasses – he chose bright blue – which made him look quite distinguished. Back at school, everyone started calling him "Little Doctor" since he looked like such a scholar, a nickname he embraced so fully that he asked his teachers to use it every time they called on him.

Each time I see Sterling's updated reports, I realize that if we wouldn't have been flexible in our definition of foster care, we would have lost our ability to provide him with the extra services he needs. We would also have missed the opportunity to advocate for all of the children who are now able to remain in our care. I'm grateful for the compromise.

Our work around the world has taught me repeatedly that this complex life is always subject to change. We sometimes must adapt to survive, even when we wish that weren't the case. What matters the most to us at LWB, however, is making sure as many children as possible know their lives have value. If that means adjusting our plans when those inevitable fir trees fall down to block our path, then that's what we'll do. Just like the ancient Dong love songs, lifted to the sky with hope, we know the deep human need for connection. It's why we'll never stop working to ensure even more vulnerable children receive the care and nurturing they deserve.

The Heart of Community

Chapter 8: Kindness

Every person in the world should be kind to each other. As humans, we should help from our hearts.

Kin Thida, LWB-Cambodia Primary School Teacher

When LWB first began helping children in China, I made a lot of trips back and forth from the US to a city on the eastern coast of Guangdong Province. I always stayed at the same hotel, as it was located close to the orphanage. It was on my second trip that I met a young bellboy named Ao. He was just 18 years old, and he was fascinated that someone had flown 8,000 miles to work in the city's orphanage. At the time, there were only 12 foreigners out of the five million people who lived in the city, so Ao was excited to have the opportunity to practice his English. He asked so many questions about my work, my children, and life in America. Every time I would come into the hotel, he would run over to speak with me, calling out "Hello, Ms. Amy Eldridge!"

With each subsequent trip, we became better friends, and I always looked forward to seeing him. In 2004, when Ao was 19, he was promoted to bell captain. He was so proud of his new uniform, spinning in front of me with his arms outstretched so I could see every formal detail. It was wonderful to always have such a welcoming, smiling face at the hotel when I would return from the orphanage, often at extremely late hours.

In *The Heart of an Orphan*, I wrote about LWB's very first cleft trip to China, which was held at the #2 Affiliated Hospital of Shantou University in May 2004. Orphanages throughout the province had brought their children to be healed by our medical team, and over 50 cleft surgeries were done during that special week. During that trip, Ao was especially kind to me. He knew I was working 18-hour days, and no matter when I would return to the hotel, he would send fresh fruit to my room. I didn't get a chance to see him very much on that trip because the team's schedule was just so busy, but I would still occasionally hear "Hello, Ms. Amy Eldridge!" shouted across the lobby as I came and went.

I did not return to the city until October that year, but Ao was the first to welcome me at the hotel. He came running up to me in the lobby with a bag he had saved for me for six months. Inside were surgical scrubs that our team had worn back in the spring. He had sent them to be laundered, folding them all up and placing them in the back office, just waiting for the day that "Ms. Amy Eldridge" would come back to claim them. The first thing I noticed on this trip was that he had on a sport coat. He proudly told me that he was the new night manager of the hotel, just after celebrating his 20th birthday. His English was becoming better and better, and he told me that he was teaching himself with an English dictionary for long hours at a time.

One night I brought back some of the teenage girls from the orphanage for a quick visit, and he had them all in giggles as he escorted them to the elevator and then bowed and waved us in. He asked, "And these young ladies are...?" I smiled and replied, "My very good friends." He gave an even deeper bow and said, "Then warmest welcome to you ladies," which had the girls in an absolute titter.

A few days before I left on a trip in 2005, I got an email from Ao that he had seen my name on the reservation list and that he had a surprise for me when I arrived. He warmly welcomed me back to Shantou and took me up to a new room that they had just finished painting the day before. He was so proud that he had installed an in-room computer modem for me to use, as before I had always spent time in the hotel business center. He said, "Ms. Amy Eldridge is always so busy, and so I wanted to make your job better." I never had the heart to tell him that I didn't own a laptop at the time. He was so happy that he had been able to do something in friendship to make my life easier while I was there.

Before I left for China on my next trip, I realized how very much I looked forward to seeing this young man who always had a smile on his face and who always welcomed me back in such a warm way. So, I went out shopping for him, and I found a beautiful blue and silver pen that was simple but elegant. I could just imagine Ao using it in his work. It was not expensive...not at all...but I had fun shopping for him.

When I arrived, I immediately noticed that Ao now had on a full suit, and he came hurrying over to do a full turn so I could take in his newest uniform. He then proudly presented me with his business card, which said "Assistant Manager." I did a pretty Oklahoman thing and gave out a loud "Woohoo!", which made everyone in the lobby turn to stare at us.

During my few days in Shantou, there were several times that Ao came to find me to talk, and suddenly I realized that he always asked about MY work, and I knew so little about his. I asked him if he would be willing to tell me his life story. He explained that he was from the far north of China, in a place I wouldn't know. I smiled and said, "Try me." He said he was from Dalian, in a small town called Siping. When I said, "I know that area...there is an orphanage there," he couldn't believe it. He had no idea that there was an orphanage in his own hometown.

Ao told me that the area where he grew up was extremely poor, and he sadly shared that his father had died when he was very young. After Ao's father's death, the family struggled to survive. His mom was in poor health, and so at the age of 16 he dropped out of school and decided he had to become a man and support his mother. He knew he would have to leave his small town to find work, but he was determined to earn enough money to relieve his mom's stress. The young teen bid a tearful goodbye to his mom and got on a train, with no clear idea of where he was going. He rode on the train for 53 hours straight before making the decision to get off in Shantou.

For six months he tried to find work with no luck, but finally... FINALLY...he was hired at the local hotel as a bellboy. Ao said he worked as hard as possible so that he could send money back to his mother, and his determination and diligence paid off, with promotions to bell captain, night manager, and then assistant manager. I said that his mother must be so immensely proud of him, and he smiled and said she was. I was proud of him, too...traveling 53 hours on a train to find his fortune, and then working night and day to try and make a better life for his mom.

My last night in Shantou, I told him I had a gift for him. He was speechless and said he could not accept, but I just smiled and replied that it was such a little gift that he had to take it. As I handed him the box with the blue and silver pen, I said again, "Really, it is such a small gift, but I had so much fun thinking of you while choosing it." And then Ao, this young man who had lived the last four years on his own, told me he had no present for me in return. He said quietly, "Perhaps you would accept a story as my gift?"

He then apologized if his English wasn't perfect and proceeded to tell me an old Chinese tale from Dalian. It was the story of a simple peasant and a truly kind emperor, who did great things for the people of China. The peasant wanted to give the emperor a gift, but he had no money at all to do so. One day as he was walking outside, the man saw a beautiful golden bird. Its feathers sparkled in the sunshine. The man wanted to give it to the emperor so badly. He worked continually trying to catch it, to no avail. One day, however, he finally succeeded, and he held onto the golden bird with all his might.

The man then started a long journey to see the emperor. He walked and walked under the hot sun and over mountains, all the while cradling the beautiful golden bird. He was so happy and excited to know he had such a fitting gift for the king. It was an exhausting journey. Right before the peasant got to the emperor's home, he was so weak from walking that he relaxed his grip on the bird for just a moment, and it quickly flew away. The man jumped and tried to catch the bird, but he was only able to grasp one golden tail feather. Saddened, he continued his journey to the emperor's home and saw a long line of people lining up to bring gifts. The people around him all laughed at what he held. "Who would think a bird feather is fit for a king?", they asked.

Finally, it was the peasant's turn, and he humbly went up to the emperor holding the single feather. He told the king, "I had wanted to bring you a golden bird like the sun, but the bird escaped my hands. And so, I bring you a gift that I know is not grand. But please, kind king, know that this simple gift carries with it all of my love, and I give it to you with all of my heart."

By then, Ao was standing in the hallway with tears streaming down his face. He said, "Ms. Amy Eldridge, I give you this story with my whole heart because you were the very first friend I felt I had in Shantou."

Somehow, I managed to get back inside my room before crying. The next day he was at the manager's desk smiling his regular huge smile, calling out, "Hello Ms. Amy Eldridge!", while taking his new pen from his suit coat pocket and waving it at me. It was very hard to say goodbye to him this time, because I already knew my next trips to China for at least 18 months would not have me returning to Shantou. I would miss seeing my friend.

Far too often, our news and social media try their best to divide us. I read a recent article that said almost 90% of the news that is reported in the US has a negative take. Convincing us that our world is breaking down from the danger of "us" versus "them" definitely sells more papers. I have yet to go anywhere in the world, however, where I haven't met incredibly warm people who love to spend time one on one, talking about their lives and their families. Wonderful people just like Ao, who often have so little and yet live with such kindness and grace that it humbles my soul.

I will never forget the gift of Ao's story because he shared it with such sincerity. It has nothing to do with how much a gift costs, does it? It has everything to do with your heart. You cannot measure the worth of something given with such genuine kindness, because receiving such a gift means we get to experience such a beautiful part of humanity…simply loving one another.

One of the biggest blessings of the work I get to do each day is that we continually get to see goodness and graciousness poured out to help those who are hurting.

When COVID-19 was first declared a pandemic, we honestly didn't know what would happen with our donations. Many of our supporters were in industries that had to shut down, and the whole world had such an enormous feeling of uncertainty. I know everyone reading this book will remember how they were feeling in March and April of 2020 as the economies of almost every country began to decline. We watched as food lines grew and unemployment skyrocketed. For those of us who work with children in low-income areas, we knew the economic crisis triggered by COVID would pose a grave risk to their very health and survival.

Shortly after COVID became a global emergency, one of the most respected medical journals, *The Lancet*, published an article on the rise of child malnutrition in low-income countries due to the pandemic. The article stated, "Without adequate action, the profound impact of the COVID-19 pandemic on early life nutrition could have intergenerational consequences for child growth and development and life-long impacts on education, chronic disease risks, and overall human capital formation." At the same time, a projection from the World Food Programme stated that the number of people facing acute hunger during the pandemic would increase from 130 million to 265 million.

The articles only confirmed what we were already seeing in the rural regions where we work. The food situation for children in countries like Cambodia and Uganda was reaching a crisis level under lockdown. We knew we had to take action, and so we reached out to our supporters to let them know we would be mobilizing teams on the ground to provide emergency food relief. We asked them to please consider making a $40 donation to feed a family impacted by COVID for an entire month, knowing that if we could feed even 100 families, we would be doing our small part to help during the crisis. The LWB community responded with such overwhelming kindness that it honestly took our breath away.

During the remainder of 2020, we were able to deliver over 485,000 pounds of food to hurting families and orphanages, helping 36,000 people receive essential nutrition. So many of their stories were just so difficult to hear. The food delivery days were always very emotional ones for our team, as each time they would head further out into the countryside to find the families who were trying desperately to survive. I could fill an entire book with their stories, but there are a few I will carry in my heart forever.

In Cambodia, the issue of unexploded landmines remains to this day. In fact, the Cambodian Mine Action Centre estimates that there may be as many as four to six million mines and explosives still buried in Cambodia's countryside. These mines, designed to target human beings, were buried throughout Cambodia by both sides during the long civil war. They can be triggered in several different ways, but most commonly they are detonated when stepped on unknowingly by an adult or young child.

Whenever I travel to Cambodia, we are reminded to "not step off the path" when visiting homes in the jungle. While many villages have worked hard to mark each unexploded mine with a red sign having a white skull-and-crossbones on it, in some of the regions along the border with Thailand, the only way someone knows there is a mine is when they hear the awful, unmistakable sound of someone stepping on one. It is estimated that Cambodia would need at least $377 million to clear the remaining mines in the country.

When COVID closed the border between Cambodia and Thailand, the official immigration checkpoints were shut and secured. The normal migration of day laborers from Cambodia came to a sudden and complete halt. Thousands of families who depended on subsistence work crossing into Thailand went from earning a few dollars a day to absolutely nothing.

Elva and her husband John had traveled to the Cambodian border hoping to find a way for him to make it into Thailand for work. They were caring for eight small children, including 6-month-old baby Jennifer. With no income whatsoever, their children were beginning to starve. John knew he had to find a way to get food for his children, so he made the decision to try to cross the border into Thailand several miles away from the now closed checkpoints. Shortly after saying goodbye to his wife in the early morning, he was killed instantly when he detonated an unmarked mine.

Elva was left with absolutely nothing. No income and no home. When our food relief team first arrived in the area, LWB director Leng recalls, "We saw a small tent shelter in the distance, and I originally thought it must be for raising chickens. When I learned it was where a widow and eight children were living, exposed to the elements, I couldn't stop my tears. I saw a little baby wrapped in a red piece of cloth. She was so skinny and malnourished. The baby had reached a point where she had used up all her energy. Mom said that her baby rarely smiled and weakly cried most of the day from hunger."

We knew we had to step forward and help immediately, so we gave Elva and the children emergency food rations for the short term. We also knew, however, that this vulnerable family, living so exposed on the border, was at high risk for trafficking and exploitation. We wanted the children to have the best opportunity of a new start following the tragic death of their father. In order to best track the children's development, we spoke with Elva to see if she would be interested in moving to one of the villages where LWB has ongoing programs. She agreed with such relief, and soon after our LWB tuk-tuk driver went to pick up the family and their meager possessions.

We had a very special surprise in store for this still heartbroken family. Thanks to LWB supporters who learned of their plight, we were able to build Elva and her children a small, safe home of their very own in Sokhem Village. When Elva heard the news, she broke down crying and expressed her deep gratitude to everyone who sent love and support for her family. The kids told us they were excited to not have to sleep on the ground any longer and to have a home that was clean and dry.

The older children shared with us that they had always dreamed of someday getting to go to school. The wonderful part about their relocation to Sokhem Village was that our education program in that area serves children from infancy through primary school. All of Elva's children were immediately enrolled in our classes, and it was a proud and special day when they finally received their very first school uniforms.

Baby Jennifer got to enroll officially in LWB school as well — at our Sokhem Early Childhood Development Center. She had ready access to lots and LOTS of good nutrition, and everything about her health and demeanor soon changed. By 9 months of age, the once malnourished baby was trying to stand on her own and even take a few tentative steps. She loved coming to school each day and interacting with the other babies and toddlers.

As for mom Elva, LWB was able to hire her as a nanny at the childhood center, so she now has a steady job and the resources to provide food for her family. She loves her work helping to feed and bathe the children in the program and making sure they are warm and safe during naptime. And, of course, she loves knowing that her own baby girl is getting all the care and attention she needs to thrive.

I'm so thankful that our team in Cambodia came upon this family while delivering emergency food to those severely impacted by COVID-19. For Baby Jennifer and her older siblings, gone are the days of the unprotected tent and deep, gnawing hunger. Instead, theirs is another powerful story of hope, made possible by the kindness of the LWB community.

When LWB first began projects for children in Africa, one of our primary goals was the establishment of foster care. Sadly, in Uganda, as in far too many other countries around the world, the orphanage business is booming. One data set I've seen stated that the number of children growing up in orphanages in Uganda alone has increased from 1,000 children in the 1990s to over 50,000 today.

It's a complicated topic. I know that lots of people with really good intentions saw what they felt was a pressing need to provide food and shelter to children who were hungry or abandoned, and the simplest solution to the problem was often, "Let's build an orphanage." It's still the solution I hear frequently when talking with mission groups or churches who support projects overseas. *"We're building an orphanage in Haiti,"* or *"You should connect with this amazing man starting an orphanage in Vietnam."*

When you start to look deeper, however, you quickly discover a sobering reality surrounding many private orphanages operating around the world. Orphans bring in funding. Lots and lots of funding. And the more orphans you have in your care, the more money you can raise from people wanting to help children. Over the last few decades, this has led to a new industry of building orphanages in lower income countries. Sadly, some very unscrupulous people often join in on the action. We receive emails almost daily from groups around the world who know the exact wording to put in their pleas to get money sent their way, with the word "orphan" always used as many times as possible to pull on the recipient's heartstrings. In far too many of these private "baby homes," the children are an income-generating activity, as the owners know that good-hearted people around the world respond generously with their gifts when they think a child has been left on their own.

I remember the very first time I visited Uganda and spoke to some village leaders in the southwest part of the country. I mentioned an orphanage in their region I had seen online. The head of the orphanage was actively recruiting volunteers on social media to come work in his facility and was doing a lot of heavy marketing to tourists who were coming to visit the gorillas. The photos he used were heart wrenching, of children in torn clothing peering at the camera with somber eyes. He described crumbling building conditions and children sleeping on the floor. "Do you know this orphanage?" I asked my new friends, but all they would say was yes, they did. I could tell they were holding back, so we quickly moved to a different topic.

The next day, we had gone into the nearest town and were having lunch together when a shiny black Land Rover came cruising down the street. When the driver parked and got out of the luxury SUV, I saw he was dressed to the nines, with a gold watch around his wrist and fancy leather shoes. In such an impoverished town, he definitely stood out. I couldn't help asking, "What does HE do for a living?" My friends exchanged glances with each other before responding, "Remember the orphanage you were asking us about yesterday? The one that gets so many foreign visitors and donations? That man is the director. The orphan business is treating him well."

It obviously was, indeed. I wish I could say it was the only time I saw shrewd hustlers profit from setting up an orphanage, but alas it is not. I still have a photo from a private orphanage who had asked for our help in southern China. When the image was first sent to me, my heart did a thousand little flips. My emotional gut instinct was, "Oh my gosh, we've got to help these children." The "pastor" who ran it had lined up about two dozen babies and toddlers in little bamboo chairs in front of a damp wall that was caving in. Their little cheeks were chapped red, and each tiny girl looked more pitiful than the next. I soon found out that the same image was being circulated online to multiple charities, all with the identical "save our starving orphans" plea. I know many groups who gave. Thankfully, it didn't take our director in that province long to do some investigative work and discover that the orphanage had several church congregations in the US supporting the children with significant donations. Very little of the funding ever reached the kids. They continued to live without heat in a dilapidated building, while the couple running the facility built a literal mansion next door.

Herein lies a very real problem. As well-meaning but often misinformed groups around the world send in foreign dollars to support destitute children living in institutions, the numbers of "orphans" entering these facilities often begins rising. I put the word "orphans" in quotation marks because far fewer children around the world than you might think actually fit the classic definition of that word. Those who know me well know the oft used statistic of 143 million orphans in the world gets me riled up. When most people hear a child is an orphan, their minds automatically assume that he or she has either lost their parents through death or abandonment. They imagine a child completely alone and forlorn. It's certainly the image that came to my mind when I first got involved in adoption and then working overseas. I now know how very naive I was when I first wanted to help as well.

The reality about this staggering number of orphaned children is a far different story, as the enormous figure above includes what UNICEF defines as "single orphans," or children who have had one parent pass away. This means that a child who had a parent die but who is still living with a devoted mother or father is technically declared an orphan and included in the 143 million statistic. I struggle with this definition as a single mom myself, and I wish that the word "vulnerable" to describe these children who have lost a parent would be used in its place. UNICEF states right on their website that they created this definition during the 1990s in order to capture all those children who had a parent die from the AIDS crisis that was sweeping across Africa.

It was a devastating time period, and I know that millions of children were left in desperate situations. The orphan definition, however, often paints a false picture in many people's minds, as they automatically think of orphans as requiring care and shelter, perhaps in an institution, and then ultimately needing adoption as well. Each time I see "143 million orphans" on any adoption agency website, my blood pressure begins to rise. That number should never be used to insinuate that there are that many children around the world needing new, permanent homes. What the vast majority of these children need instead is family strengthening and community support. For reasons I still don't fully understand, though, these types of projects rarely fund as well as direct orphanage support, even though most children living right now in orphanages have families who are known.

There are lots of reasons why children with living parents end up in private orphanages. Many times, a mom or dad has sent their child to live in an institution with the promise of free food and education. As I've mentioned, I've visited too many facilities where those promises are never delivered, as keeping the children in sad conditions ensures the donations will keep flowing.

Other parents place their children into orphanage care after they divorce and remarry. We frequently see children in Uganda and Cambodia brought to live in institutions when their new stepparents simply don't want them around. One of the most tragic reasons why children are often surrendered to orphanage care, however, is that their parents, who most often care deeply about them, simply don't have enough money to feed them. These are children who really weigh on my heart, as poverty should never be a reason why parents and children who love each other are separated. Yet it's a story we hear repeatedly.

Thankfully, there is an increasing movement around the world to deinstitutionalize children, which LWB has supported since 2004 through our work with family-based care. Just as we had been in China and Cambodia, we were committed to helping as many children as possible in Uganda grow up in families versus institutions as well. In the summer of 2017, we were able to move a first group of children from an orphanage in southern Uganda into foster care in the surrounding community. It has been an enormously impactful program, thanks to our committed staff on the ground who do everything in their power to find the exact right placement for each child.

For many of the children, the right placement actually means being reunified with their biological parents or extended family. Those are celebrations that come after an incredible amount of work being done by LWB social workers, local village leaders, and government officers. Our social workers serve not only as case managers for the legal care orders of the children but also as private detectives. They often travel long distances to remote regions of the country, following up on every lead to track down parents, aunts and uncles, or adult siblings. The primary goal is to determine exactly why a child is living in orphanage care in the first place and then to decide how to safely transition the child out of an orphanage and into family-based care.

When we first began working with orphanages in Uganda, we soon realized that most of the children we were working with could return to their birth families if given the proper support. Every child's case is completely unique, just like the reason they ended up in an orphanage in the first place. This means that the solution for every child to leave institutional care must be uniquely personalized as well.

In 2019, we became involved with 6-year-old Shirley, whose mom had surrendered her to a local orphanage after her husband had abandoned the family. The mom only had enough income to feed the infant and an older brother, and so Shirley was sent away. After multiple home visits and assessments, our team was confident that poverty was the only reason this family was not united. Instead of being with her mom and her two siblings, Shirley was instead sleeping in an orphanage room in a long row of metal bunkbeds. She cried frequently and even ran away from the orphanage several times searching for her mother. The mom would cry each time she brought the little girl back to the welfare home, apologizing for not having enough money to feed three children as a single mother.

With an $1,800 investment, we were able to help Shirley's mom set up a small shop to sell food items in her town. The simple kiosk was stocked with items like beans and fresh fruit, and in the very first month of business Shirley's mother turned a profit. Over the next few months, the little store continued to do a brisk business, and soon Shirley's mom had her very first savings account. You can imagine what a wonderful day it was when Shirley was able to leave the orphanage behind for good. This beautiful little girl now gets to grow up where she belongs, with a mom who deeply loves her. While some might feel that investing $1,800 into an income-generating project for an adult doesn't qualify as "orphan care," we know that one of the greatest things we can ever do for a child in an orphanage is finding a way for them to return home.

We have also had situations in Uganda where children are kept from their birth families because it's felt that the orphanage is a safer building than some of the crumbling homes out in the countryside or in the crowded cities. We helped with one little boy who had spent years in an orphanage, despite his grandmother desperately wanting to care for him, because her house was built over an open sewer. Everyone from the probation office to the orphanage director knew this grandma adored her grandson. But once again, the cruelty of poverty had kept little Micah from being in family care. Over the years, he had many overseas donors who had been willing to support his monthly costs in the orphanage, but no one had stepped forward to fund uniting him with a family member. We were overjoyed when a kind supporter said they would donate $5,000 to build the grandmother a small home, and Micah is now thriving in her care. It shows that by making an investment to strengthen a family's situation, children living in orphanages can often return to their villages. In one orphanage alone, we were able to safely reunify almost 50 children with their birth parents or extended family members.

Of course, not all children can go home. There are very real cases of neglect and abuse, and sadly times where both parents do pass away. This is when we believe so strongly in foster care versus the "easier" route of simply sending a child to an orphanage. Every child deserves a family to love them. Thankfully, the government of Uganda now openly recognizes that children deserve families and not institutions, and so there is a major effort underway to increase the number of foster care placements. Finding available and willing families still remains a challenge, however, because many families in Uganda are already caring for children in addition to their own. "Fostering" your nieces or nephews or grandchildren is part of Ugandan culture, so for many people, they truly aren't able to add in another child.

We have certainly identified some amazing foster parents, though. It has been a slow but steady process, one child at a time, and we cheer each time a secure placement is made that keeps a child from growing up in an orphanage. We've seen several domestic adoptions arise from foster care now as well, which is always a true joy. One of my favorite outcomes involves a little girl named Tabitha, who entered an orphanage after being found abandoned with HIV. She actually went through the international adoption process originally, as at the time it was commonly thought that the only way a child with HIV would ever find a permanent home was by being chosen by a family overseas.

Uganda's adoption laws at that time required international adopters to move to Uganda and foster the child for a one-year period, so Tabitha's prospective adoptive family moved from their home in Texas to the capital city of Kampala. Tabitha was placed with them the very next week. After just a short time in-country, however, the parents decided not to complete the adoption.

We were relieved that the orphanage director then agreed that Tabitha could go into LWB foster care instead of returning to the orphanage. Tabitha was placed with a kind Ugandan woman who herself had HIV, which she controlled well with medication. As a single woman, she had never had children, and she welcomed Tabitha into her life with her arms thrown open. With each new report, we could clearly see that she had fallen completely in love with this wonderful little girl. After a year of having Tabitha in her home, we were thrilled when the foster mom told us she was beginning the process to legally make Tabitha her daughter. It was the happy ending…and new beginning…they both deserved.

In early 2021, we held our first conference on foster care in the city of Mukono to help more families in the community learn about this essential model of child welfare. I'm excited to see family-based care in Uganda continue to expand, and I hope that in the next five years we will see more orphanages begin to close as the number of foster families continues to rise.

When I think of the beautiful children who are currently in LWB foster care, I immediately pull up an image of a little girl in an oversized cream dress dotted with tiny flowers. She is posing with her hand on her hip and the most amazing smile. I always think of Charlotte, who so easily could have been lost to the institutional system, but who is now thriving with the love and support of her village.

Charlotte was born with cerebral palsy, which impacted both her arms and legs. Because of her medical condition, she struggled to walk with a normal gait or to hold items easily in her hand. Her mouth was also affected, making speech difficult and leading her to drool, which unfortunately carries an enormous social stigma.

Charlotte had been brought to an orphanage following the death of her mother, when her overwhelmed father felt he couldn't handle her care on his own. She lived in the orphanage for several years until her dad decided to remarry and bring his daughter back home. Everyone was so hopeful for Charlotte, but it quickly became clear that her stepmother resented having a child with special needs in her newly married life. When the social worker went to visit Charlotte at home one day, the father admitted that his new wife had been abusing the little girl, denying her food because of her physical disabilities. In desperation, the dad had asked a neighbor to temporarily care for Charlotte, and the family had agreed since they were all from the same tribe.

    The social worker then went to see Charlotte at the neighbor's house, and her heart was saddened to see a little girl who had clearly lost weight from the mistreatment by her stepmom. It was also obvious, however, in watching Charlotte and her father together, that the dad truly loved his little girl. Could a solution be found to keep him in her life while also providing the safety and security that little Charlotte deserved?

    Charlotte entered LWB foster care in early 2018 in the same village as her father but with a local family who absolutely embraced her, regardless of her special needs. The foster mom has such a gentle tenderness about her, and what we love about Charlotte's home is that she now has several foster siblings, who are loving and kind to her as well. The girls love being together, playing everything from dolls to an active game of dodgeball. The neighborhood children have also accepted Charlotte in a beautiful way, cheering her on as she takes part in their games, albeit more slowly. Charlotte's birth father stops by the foster home frequently, and the bond between the two of them remains strong. While we know it's a complicated situation, the important thing we focus on is that everyone in Charlotte's life right now simply wants the best for this sweet little girl.

    Before LWB's involvement, Charlotte never had the opportunity to attend school; so as soon as she was placed into a foster home, we began exploring possibilities for her to receive an education. While there are several schools in the region for children with special needs, we were hopeful that Charlotte could attend the same local primary school as her foster sisters. We were thrilled when the principal was willing to try, and Charlotte was enrolled at the age of 10 in what they called the "baby class," since she had never had formal schooling in the past. The first few weeks were difficult at times, as Charlotte would get extremely frustrated when the teacher and other students were unable to understand her speech. The weakness in her hands also made it difficult for her to write the alphabet. Thankfully, whenever Charlotte would get upset, her foster sisters would immediately come over to help calm her.

    We knew that Charlotte had been through so many difficult changes in her life, from moving in and out of orphanage care to being separated again from her father. Add to the mix starting school for the first time, and we all understood how completely overwhelmed she must feel. We asked an LWB volunteer who specializes in trauma to give some suggestions and advice to Charlotte's teacher, and it was wonderful to see how calm and gentle the teacher was whenever Charlotte began to struggle.

    By the very next month, Charlotte adored going to school. And by the end of the first term, she had received high marks in both reading and math. She had also made many new friends. This incredibly bright little girl had helped show everyone that being born with a special need doesn't have to limit one's future. Charlotte was promoted to the mid-level class, and we couldn't have been prouder. It was then that we saw yet again how a simple act of kindness can make such an enormous difference in another person's life.

    Charlotte was so excited to be part of the older class, and she loved dressing each day in her beautiful red and white school uniform. She was always very careful to keep her dress and sweater clean and tidy. As I mentioned earlier, Charlotte's cerebral palsy causes her to drool, which is a side effect for about 30% of people who are born with this condition. The drooling distressed Charlotte greatly, however, when wearing her school uniform, as she always wanted it to stay neat. When her new teacher saw how upsetting this was to Charlotte, she came up with a wonderful idea. She took scrap material the same color as the red in the school uniform and sewed several small aprons. Charlotte could now wear a matching apron over her dress and change it out whenever it got wet. This simple act of kindness had a huge impact on a little girl who cherished going to school. One of my favorite photos of Charlotte shows her confidently standing in front of a brick building in her red dress and apron, ready to head to class with a smile like sunshine.

When we first started our foster care work in Uganda, we were frequently told that it would only be possible to find foster families for children who were "healthy." I am so glad we didn't listen to those voices saying that foster care for children with special needs could not be done, as we're doing it every day with remarkable impact. Peace Okong, Charlotte's social worker, sums it up beautifully: "At the orphanage, Charlotte didn't have a sense of belonging. But now she is proud that she has a family of her own to care for her. She has experienced so much love and affection from her family that no orphanage in the world can give." Charlotte shows that with the right foster placement, every child can experience quality, home-based care. And with a supportive community…of friends, teachers, and neighbors…children truly thrive.

I consider myself so fortunate to be part of an international community that actively seeks to spread kindness to people all over the world. I have always loved that our community truly celebrates the children in our programs, as one of our essential core values is that when a child comes into our hands, we want them to feel valued. I want them to leave our care knowing how much we believe in them. One of the special things we are seeing now that we've been a charity for almost two decades is that kids we helped back at the beginning of LWB are now reaching adulthood and choosing to volunteer and donate to us. We get cards and texts that say things like, *"I'll never forget how LWB made me feel…and I want to pay that forward."* These are moments that fill my heart with joy, as they show that kindness has an amazing way of being received by one person and then passed on to another. I get to see those ripples daily. Since sowing kindness doesn't have to cost a single penny, every human on earth can add their measure.

There is space for everyone who wants to do good on this earth. While sometimes it might seem like only celebrities and the most famous nonprofits are deemed worthy to make the news for their charitable giving, the reality is that all around us kind-hearted people and organizations are creating moments that never make the headlines. Moments that bring love and mercy and goodness into a world which needs it so desperately.

In the work that we do, it is difficult to pick just a few key stories to illustrate the inner beauty which comes from kindness, but I can't close this chapter without sharing one which took place on our cleft trip to Kaifeng, China. We had assembled an incredible team from the US that year, and we had children coming from orphanages throughout the mainland to receive their life-changing operations. There were two children on the surgery schedule, both with very complex medical needs, whom we will carry in our hearts forever.

Henry and Celia were from an orphanage located in a province on China's east coast. Celia had been born with a condition known as microphthalmia, where the eyeballs are malformed and extremely small. In Celia's case, it had left her blind in one eye. She also had an extremely wide bilateral cleft lip and palate. Since she was 4 years old and had not had her cleft lip repaired yet, her permanent teeth were coming out of the tissue between her nostrils. It was going to be a complicated repair.

Her best friend Henry was 6 years old and had bilateral Tessier number seven cleft, an extremely rare condition. While most people who hear the word "cleft" automatically think of the most common fissure in the lip, the medical definition of cleft refers to any gap in a child's soft tissue, bone, or both. Some clefts involve not only the mouth and nose but other parts of the face as well. In 1976, the famous French surgeon Paul Tessier classified 15 different types of cleft. In Henry's case, his cleft extended on either side of his mouth all the way up to his cheekbones.

Henry's nannies had told us that he was very self-conscious about his facial difference because sadly he had faced so much open ridicule about his appearance. Despite the bullying, his nannies said that Henry was a truly kind little boy, who gladly helped them out with chores. They also described him as very tender-hearted toward the younger kids in his orphanage. Henry would always try and comfort the little ones around him when they were crying. We were so thankful that both Henry and Celia would soon be able to meet with our medical team.

It was a very emotional moment for every LWB volunteer on the hospital floor when Henry and Celia finally arrived. They were both wearing face masks (pre-pandemic!), and at first we couldn't figure out why the nannies were making the children cover their faces. They quickly explained that since the children had such complex facial issues, the adults in the orphanage never took the children outside. They had to travel by train on this day, however, to get to Kaifeng, and they knew the children would be subjected to a lot of negative comments if their faces were seen. Because of this, they decided the children needed to wear masks the entire way.

Several on our team admitted later that they were originally upset that anyone would feel a child with cleft had to be "hidden," but very quickly we realized how compassionate the caregivers were actually being by taking this extra precaution. As soon as the kids' masks were removed, other families in the hospital gasped and began coming over to stare. One woman cleaning the hospital became so vocally upset that the children began to cry.

As quickly as we could, our team began taping paper over the hospital room windows so no one could see inside. But as news spread about the children, families from other floors began coming to look, even ripping the papers down so they could gawk at the kids. Thankfully, the hospital staff got involved and helped secure the room, and the protective papers were put back up to cover the windows. It was a moment we never anticipated, and it took time to get it under control. Thankfully, once the paper was back up and the door was firmly closed, the children were able to be calmed and began warming up to our team.

Henry began to have fun pretty quickly after the crowd was dispersed. He loved building 3D puzzles and playing with the cars and balls we had brought. And Celia was just the sweetest. It was wonderful to see how tender Henry was with her. He would frequently sit beside her with his arm around her side, encouraging her that everything was going to be alright. When Henry figured out that we had a room down the hallway where the toys for the week were being kept, he worked up the courage to go down the hall to pick some toys for Celia and himself. Of course, our team couldn't refuse him no matter how many times he came back.

Celia was scheduled for surgery the next day. She was so brave when it was time to be taken to the operating room, heading through the swinging doors with the biggest smile on her face. Her case was a difficult one, as her bilateral cleft was just so wide, but thankfully she came out of surgery well. That whole morning, Henry sat in the hospital bed very subdued, clearly worried about his little friend. Several hours later, when she was finally brought back to the ward, he took her hand and said quietly, *"Mei nu,"* whispering to Celia that she was a "beautiful girl."

As kind as Henry was, he was understandably scared as well. He was such a smart little boy who had seen the other kids before him leave for the OR and then return in pain. When he learned that his surgery was now scheduled for the next day, he became quite anxious. Both surgeons on the LWB team would be operating together on Henry, since his type of facial cleft was so very rare.

Early the next morning it was time for Henry's case to begin. When the nurses came to take him downstairs to the operating area, he was waving to everyone when he left the room. Understandably, when he got down to the pre-op area, he got very nervous and began to cry. Thankfully, one of the anesthesiologists on our team was Dr. Kathy Clinch, an incredibly compassionate physician, who had traveled with LWB many times. She always did everything possible to make the kids feel comfortable and secure in the OR while administering the anesthesia before surgery. Because of Henry's facial difference, she quickly realized that the anesthesia mask in the operating room would not fit over his mouth correctly.

Dr. Clinch quickly cradled Henry in her arms and began softly singing to him. As she rocked him back and forth, she used her hands to cover both sides of the mask as best she could, so that the anesthesia could be breathed in to help him gently fall asleep. Our team photographer happened to be in the OR at that time, and the image captured of Dr. Clinch tenderly comforting Henry as he went to sleep will always bring me to tears. It was a moment of grace that sums up everything I want our charity to be.

Once the operation got underway, the surgeons determined that there was actually a 1.5-inch difference in Henry's jaw. In order for him to get the best result, he would need to first have extensive work done on that area, possibly through orthodontics or by breaking and wiring the jaw. Since that would be impossible on a one-week surgery exchange, the doctors adapted their plans to work mainly on the openings in his cheeks. Their goal was to make his face look smoother and not "gape," so it wouldn't be as alarming to people who would see him. We hoped this would help him get through a future adoption with fewer public incidents like the one which happened the day he arrived. While Henry's facial cleft wasn't completely "fixed," everyone who saw him post-surgery said his appearance was greatly improved.

Over the next few days, Henry's sweet personality returned. Once he was able to begin eating again, he had a pretty remarkable surprise in store. Before he had surgery, he always had a difficult time eating as it was hard to get food to stay in his mouth because of his wide facial cleft. You should have seen his eyes when he realized that he could now put food into his mouth and have it stay there without falling out!

We also realized one afternoon that Henry still had not seen his face since the surgery, and so we asked him if he would like to see what the doctors had done. Our photographer began showing him some photos she had taken on her camera, and it was a very moving moment for the team as Henry saw his new appearance for the first time. Everyone was telling him he was so handsome, and we could see that he was very affected by the images he saw. He was usually very talkative and friendly to everyone who came by, but after seeing the difference in his appearance he didn't want to speak at all because he was afraid of hurting the delicate stitches. He wanted everything to heal perfectly. Even without speaking, however, his tender-heartedness shone through. As our medical team made the rounds, they watched as Henry quietly took Celia's hand in his. Even while being as careful as he could be to protect his own incisions, he still wanted to make sure his little friend felt comforted.

I have learned through my work that kindness doesn't roar. It often shows up in the softest and most unexpected ways, like a 6-year-old orphaned boy sitting with his arm around his friend, or a caring physician softly singing her patient to sleep. They are moments that certainly don't make the front-page news, but I know deep down we all realize they are moments that matter. When you get to experience genuine goodness from another person, it is one of the best and most beautiful gifts we can receive.

Chapter 9: Resilience

I like drawing flowers and houses filled with families who love each other. It makes me feel happy.

Safe Haven Foster Care Program Child

(Warning: this chapter discusses sexual assault)

Back in 1998, when we first decided to grow our family through adoption, I knew almost nothing about the loss and trauma that a child experiences to even reach that point. In fact, my first educational moment on adoption didn't come until I was almost 30, when I became friends with a woman who had adopted domestically. I groan now when I remember asking her one of the most common questions all adoptive families hear... *"Do you know who her real mother is?"*

I am so grateful that my friend took the time to gently educate me that, of course, she WAS her daughter's real mom. She introduced me to the words used most often in adoption, explaining that it was her daughter's biological parents who had made the decision to place her little girl with a new family. Of course both the birth and adoptive moms were very much real.

Looking back now, I am amazed that the agency we used in 1999 to facilitate our first adoption didn't require any preparatory education classes before moving forward. Not a single one. I never questioned it back then because I was already the mom of five children. I foolishly assumed that being a parent meant I was already competent enough to bring any new child into our home, even though that child was going to be a different race and from a different country. My lack of preparation the day I met my daughter in China still astonishes me, when I was unceremoniously handed an actual baby human to raise while standing in a hotel lobby.

I, of course, knew about the One Child policy and that thousands of babies were living in Chinese orphanages at the time. It's why I had learned in the first place that so many little girls were in need of permanent homes. What I didn't fully understand at the time, which now makes me feel such shame, is the deep trauma that every child who ends up in an orphanage has lived through. The abandonment certificate every adoptive parent is given as part of the formal paperwork often just lists an address where the child was found. With my daughter's permission, I can share that her paperwork simply stated that she was found in front of a bank. One little statement on a white piece of paper that in no way conveys what the first week of my daughter's life entailed.

She and I feel fortunate that many years ago I was able to speak with one of the women who had been working at a market stall by the bank the day my daughter was found. We know that someone had taken the time to wrap her carefully in a blanket before putting her in a basket. We know they cared enough to tuck a red envelope of money deep inside. I am grateful she was found quickly, although there are many more unknowns in the next seven days of her life.

We were told that a street sweeper is the one who found my daughter, after hearing her cries. As a crowd gathered to look at the screaming infant, supposedly a rich woman in the area who was passing by the bank demanded the baby be undressed to check for any special needs. When Anna was found to be a healthy newborn, an argument broke out between the wealthy woman and the street cleaner, who each wanted to take the baby for themselves. The street cleaner ultimately won through "finders keepers," and Anna was taken to her very simple home. Not to be outdone, the well-off woman notified the police that a child had been found and claimed unlawfully. One week later, Anna was removed from the cleaner's home and taken to the orphanage.

Every child's abandonment story is completely unique. Who took the child from their home and chose the exact moment and location to leave them? Was it mom or dad, an in-law, a neighbor? Was the child wanted by the parents but forced away by the in-laws? Was the abandonment a result of a special need or an inability to pay for medical care? There is often no way to know… but it remains a common occurrence. It's estimated that each year almost 100,000 children in China find themselves left on their own.

Since we went on to do so much work in my daughter's orphanage over the years, I have a fairly good understanding of what the next month of Anna's life was like. Her orphanage had an "abandonment room," where new babies and toddlers were kept until it could be determined whether they had any communicable diseases. I absolutely hated going to this part of the orphanage, because the profound grief and sorrow of the children who were taken there is something that cut to my very core. Each time I would visit, there were, of course, new children. Toddlers who were so distraught over losing their parents would stand terrified in the corner, in that awful stage of hyperventilation where their gasping sobs would mix with not breathing. The babies in that room were often not only in emotional distress but physical, after being found outside in extreme heat or cold. I saw babies covered in swollen red ant bites after being found in the grass. As I wrote about in *The Heart of an Orphan*, I even saw babies who were discovered first tragically by rats or other animals, before the police were notified.

The cruel reality of child abandonment was something that I discussed many times with an orphanage staff member who was responsible for the paperwork needed to file a child for adoption. She and one particular police officer wondered what the compassionate thing was to do when listing how and where a child was found. Everyone has different opinions, of course, on how much sorrow should be shared with a child. Many of my friends in China feel that, when it comes to difficult life experiences, it is always better to look forward than to reflect back. It's why some orphanage workers felt it was best to not even document that a child lived in an institution, rarely photographing them or keeping any sort of life history. I had more than one orphanage director tell me that they didn't understand why Western adoptive families wanted so many details about their child's past, when their sad circumstances would only bring a child pain. They felt it was far healthier to concentrate on a child's life once placed in a family, as that's when happy memories would finally be made.

To someone who really believes it is better to look forward than back, there are some abandonment stories they would never want a child to know. I'm certain that the baby girl whose foot had to be amputated after it was partially chewed off by a rat did not have that information listed in her adoption file. "Unknown amputation" was all that was noted. I remember another child abandonment I got to experience where the baby had been fished out of a river by a man in a passing boat, after someone threw the newborn off the city bridge. The family who went on to adopt that child would have read "found near the East Bridge" instead of "nearly drowned in the river," because the orphanage staff felt that was the far more compassionate thing for the baby to someday hear. What inner trauma does that now grown child still have locked inside her brain, however, after physically losing a birthmother, experiencing a long freefall from a bridge, hitting the cold, dirty water, and then almost drowning? All before ending up in an orphanage abandonment room.

I know there are many official abandonment certificates which simply state "found at the orphanage gates." It's a maddening line for so many in the adoption world who are searching for their truth, but I do understand why some kind orphanage staff I knew felt it was sometimes preferable to use that popular location rather than "found in the alley dumpster." Abandonment can't be sanitized, though, even when the real location is in the safest place possible, such as my daughter being left on the steps of a bank. Abandonment is a trauma that no child should have to experience.

When I first got the adoption referral of my daughter Anna, she was one of the youngest babies my agency had ever seen. She was only 5 months old when matched to our family, and 7 months old at adoption. I remember at the time so many people in my town said to me, "Oh, you're so lucky she's a little baby, as she won't be impacted the way an older child would be." You have to remember that I knew almost nothing about adoption life or trauma at that time, so I fully believed them.

Now, of course, I understand far too well that for many children, spending even one month in a crowded orphanage can have long-lasting effects. When well-meaning friends or even strangers say things like, "Thank goodness she got out as a baby," I do just what my new friend did all those years ago when she gently took the time to educate me about the best wording to use with adoption. If I feel they are sincere with their interest, I'll ask them to imagine what orphanage life can really be like for a newborn. Would they put their own baby in a crib for 23 hours a day, propping a bottle on a rag near her face at 8 am, 1 pm, and 6 pm, with no feedings during the night? What if I told them they could only pick up their daughter when her diaper is so filled with waste that she's screaming with discomfort? Would they want to repeat that cycle with their child every day for a year?

This was real life for tens of thousands of babies in institutional care. How does that impact a child's sense of safety and well-being? We all know the answer to that question. These are common orphanage realities that so many of us in the adoption world, myself included, wish we could somehow erase from our children's lives, but there is no magic wand for trauma.

After working with LWB for so long to help children who are often from extremely hard situations, one of the psychological traits that I ponder the most is resilience. Why can some children live through the most horrific things, even over a span of years, and somehow go on to thrive, while others experience a single trauma and battle throughout their lives to feel whole? I haven't found an answer, but what I've learned completely is that suffering is not a competition, no matter how many people try to make it so. Every individual processes their life experiences in their own unique way. Everyone experiencing pain deserves compassion, versus "Well, at least your trauma wasn't as bad as mine."

Back when international adoption was at its peak, I would get calls almost every week from parents considering the adoption of a child in our programs. Many wanted me to somehow guarantee that the child whose file they were reviewing would transition well to their family. I had learned early on that no one is able to predict which experiences will cause someone to have difficulties. There often seemed to be no rhyme or reason to how a child would integrate with a family post-adoption. I saw children who had known real abuse in institutional care embrace their new lives with relish, while some children I thought would do well after adoption really struggled to find their way. I also learned that any adoptive parent who was expecting a child to seamlessly blend into their family was most likely just as naive as I had been all those years ago.

If you'll allow me to go back one more time to my Christmas broken leg (it has to be good for something, right?), I want to point out how great it was that I could go to radiology and know within a matter of minutes what was wrong and exactly where the bone was fractured. The doctor could light up the x-ray film and point to the precise part of my body that was broken. He knew the immediate solution, assuring me that after eight weeks in a walking boot the break would be almost invisible. That knowledge of a clear diagnosis can bring a great deal of comfort when one is hurt. Why can't there be an x-ray for our emotions as well? When our hearts have been broken, there is no simple scan to say, "Here's exactly what's wrong and how you can fix it." That is where resilience must step in, allowing us to emerge from our mental pain to embrace the hope that life can get better.

Over the years, I've become the confidant of several orphaned children who were never chosen for adoption. They grew up in institutions having to process their experiences and grief often on their own. What I've learned through our discussions is that all children want to believe they are good and worthy of being loved. They NEED that in their core. When they rarely get positive affirmation in their lives, they struggle emotionally. They often battle with low self-esteem, and some even take their unknown frustrations out on those weaker than them.

One of the children I befriended many years ago, a petite and quiet girl named Dana, ended up becoming an orphanage nanny herself when she aged out of the system as an older teen. As a child, Dana had been one of the girls who was always on the periphery of any activity we planned. You could tell that part of her wanted to jump right in, but something inside her head warning her not to trust us almost always won out. She had been born with a medical need that wasn't widely accepted, and I knew that, in addition to facing negative comments from some of the orphanage caregivers, she faced bullying at school. It took a long time for her to feel comfortable talking with me, but by the time she became a young adult she seemed much more relaxed in my company.

One day when we were talking, after she had been an orphanage nanny for about two years, I told her that I was always so proud of how caring and attentive she was to the babies in her room. The simple compliment I had just spoken unexpectedly brought her to tears, which quickly turned to all out sobs. It was as if the emotional faucet to her heart had suddenly turned on, and raw grief came pouring out.

"I used to drop them," she said through her gasps. "I would drop them to make them hurt, too." Slowly, I pieced together that she was remembering when she was an older child in the orphanage, born with a special need she felt no adoptive family had wanted. She had watched as foreign families would visit the orphanage with their newly adopted children, having dressed them in fancy clothes and showered them with candy and toys. She would stand at the back of the room during their splashy visits wondering why no parents had ever found her worthy. *"Why did no one choose me?"*

Over the years, Dana's sadness turned to jealousy...and then to a simmering rage. She told me with such guilt and shame that when she would learn yet another baby had been chosen by a family, she would wait until the nanny left the room. She'd then stand at the baby's crib and either pinch them as hard as she could, or yes...even drop them onto the tile floor. She just wanted them to feel pain like she carried deep inside.

Dana then shared that having LWB team members invest into her life had made such a difference to her emotionally. Over the last few years, she had slowly come to terms with the fact that she was infinitely worthy of having a family, but that the system at the time had not allowed it. Only a certain number of children each year had been allowed to be filed from her orphanage, and that had nothing to do with how "deserving" she was of being chosen. By having someone genuinely care about her well-being, she was able to come to the realization that everything she lived through as a child, being abandoned and then growing up in a government orphanage, had been beyond her control. Finally feeling like she had permission to process what she had endured led her to know that she didn't want to make other children live through the hurt she herself had experienced. To assuage the deep, internal guilt she felt, she had quietly begun tending to the babies instead.

I don't know why that exact moment was when she felt the need to confess her hidden secret, but I was thankful that we were able to talk together openly about what every child deserves...things she hadn't received in an orphanage. She never had a mother to hold and rock her when she was sick. Or a father to help her with homework and encourage her when she struggled. She had spent her whole childhood without a family who loved her, and yet she'd survived. Finally, as a young adult, she had reached a point where she was able to focus on the good things she'd built in her life, surrounded by a few friends who truly cared about her. For Dana, daring to share with others about the complex emotions she was feeling was such an enormous first step toward finally feeling whole.

 I feel very fortunate that I get to stay in touch with many of the families whose children were helped by LWB before coming together through adoption. It's always a joy to hear from a family who says their child carries great memories of their time in our care, but of course there are so many children who only came to our attention after suffering through extremely difficult situations: malnutrition, painful medical procedures, neglect, and sadly more. Issues that don't suddenly disappear from a child's mind, no matter how kind and loving an LWB nanny might be. When I speak to parents post-adoption, many share their worries and stress over the pain their children still carry inside. Parenting a child post-trauma can be incredibly challenging, and sadly very isolating as well. Scrolling through sunny Facebook and Instagram posts can make one feel like everyone else's adoptions have unfolded like a fairy tale, when the reality is often far different. What I do see continually, however, are devoted families (despite their exhaustion), whose strength and determination to help their child come to terms with the past deserves to be honored much more than it is.

 In the early days of Love Without Boundaries, I formed a real friendship with a doctor whose heart was deeply burdened by the conditions he saw in local orphanages. He was the one who explained that only one-fourth of the orphanages in China at that time were allowed to do international adoptions. Children taken to the other more meager facilities faced even sadder outcomes. We visited many of what we called the "under orphanages," those which took overflow from the more well-known facilities, or those which were sadly dumping grounds for children abandoned with more complex needs. They were extremely difficult to visit emotionally, as we would leave knowing the children had no way out. Since many of the children had ongoing medical conditions, I knew that death was far more probable than ever having a local family show up and want to take them home.

One March day, the doctor and I visited a small orphanage that was located on the third floor of a crumbling building in a small farming river town. He had told me as we walked up the dark stairway to prepare myself for the conditions we would see. He had visited several times already, and he could only sigh and shake his head over the worry it had brought to his heart.

We knocked on the door and were brought into the orphanage's sole room, which had the unmistakable smell of urine and another foul scent. I had learned the hard way that the odor meant the children were infected with giardia, a common parasite in orphanages that causes severe and often violent diarrhea. Most of the children in the room were older, crippled with severe cerebral palsy and lying flat on their backs in metal cots. The doctor had brought me to see a baby girl who had been taken recently to the orphanage. She had a severe teratoma, a tumor on her back that had broken open and was quickly becoming infected. While my friend began his medical exam, I went bed to bed to visit the other children before stopping at a metal cot that held a little girl who couldn't have been more than 3. Her expression was one of absolute sorrow, and it pierced me to the core because it wasn't the temporary look of sadness that comes upon a toddler when they are hungry or have gotten hurt. It was a weary, defeated look of a little girl who had completely given up hoping that someone would ever be kind to her.

She was sitting on the small bed bundled up in an oversized coat. As I tried to get her to engage with me by offering a small toy and then a candy treat, nothing I presented changed her expression, and she would not meet my eye. It was like she was in her own little world, and she refused to come back to the disappointing one that was her reality. As I put my hand on her little foot, I realized that it ended shortly after her arch. When I pulled down her sock, I saw she was missing half of her left foot on one side, a special need which had most likely sentenced her to this cold room devoid of hope.

As we drove back to the city that afternoon, we discussed how to get the baby girl with the teratoma to the hospital for surgery. We then started talking about the absolute unfairness that the children from that orphanage had essentially no chance at a future, even when adoptions of children with special needs were increasingly rapidly in the United States. We both knew that there would be so many families open to adopting the little girl who was missing part of her foot, but her orphanage did not participate in the international adoption system. Shortly after, we began transferring children to the city orphanage to give them not only access to better nutrition and medical care, but also the chance for a permanent family.

When Jia was first moved from her tiny orphanage to the much larger facility, she remained completely shut down. Her nannies said she had a face that made you want to empty your pockets in an attempt to give her anything she needed. Jia only wanted to sit in her bed all day, just staring at the wall. When her nanny would pick her up and try to get her to come to the table to eat, she would crouch down in the corner and turn her face to the wall so she wouldn't have to engage with anyone. It was difficult to wonder just what she had lived through to exist completely in survival mode.

Over the next few months, Jia slowly started to form a positive relationship with one of her nannies, who patiently worked to make a clear connection. Many years later, I read a book by Parker Palmer, the founder of the Center for Courage and Renewal. It had a quote that immediately brought Jia to my mind: *"The soul is like a wild animal — tough, resilient, savvy, self-sufficient and yet exceedingly shy. If we want to see a wild animal, the last thing we should do is to go crashing through the woods, shouting for the creature to come out. But if we are willing to walk quietly into the woods and sit silently for an hour or two at the base of a tree, the creature we are waiting for may well emerge."* This was what Jia's nanny came to understand the little girl's soul most needed...to simply have someone sitting quietly next to her in kindness, letting her decide on her own when she felt safe enough to join in.

Around six months after her transfer, Jia began eating with the other children and would even sit at a small desk in our school, although she would never speak out loud. A short time later, Jia's adoption paperwork was prepared and then filed with the national authorities. Just as we expected, a family in America quickly chose her from the list of children with medical needs. I hoped her new family would contact us, as I felt it was critical that they understood just how much trauma their new daughter had experienced in her young life. I knew that Jia had many painful memories locked inside her mind and that she could easily become overwhelmed in a new, unfamiliar environment. Thankfully, during her adoption, the orphanage gave the family a note with LWB's contact information, and we were able to connect when they returned home. Hoping to give greater insight into the life experiences Jia had endured, I shared the limited amount I knew of Jia's past with her concerned mom and dad.

Fast forward 16 years, and I received a high school graduation announcement from Jia in the mail, along with a handwritten note that brought me to tears. *"I know we haven't met since China, but you are part of my past. I still feel sad at times that I can't remember more of it. I like my life now and I love my parents. I have the best family. I just want to say hi and let you know that I'm planning to be a doctor like the doctor who found me in that first orphanage. I want to help others just like people helped me."* I looked at the photo on the announcement of a vibrant, laughing teenager with long black hair and felt such a wash of emotions. I was immediately transported back to the thin and melancholy little girl who had refused to catch my eye, sitting on a metal cot in a cold and gloomy institution.

I heard from Jia's mom this past year and learned that Jia is thriving at the university she attends. She joined a sorority and is extremely active in a church college group. You would never know from her gorgeous, smiling pictures just how much she had overcome to reach a point in her life where she could shine her light on the world. It had not been an easy journey. There were long periods of sadness, anger, and even fury as she worked through the deep impact past trauma had upon her life. By having a chance at adoption and a permanent home, however, she had gained a family who absolutely refused to give up on helping her heal. Surrounded by that unconditional love, Jia found the strength to persevere.

When I think about resilience, I think first and foremost about the children in our programs who somehow find the courage to give adults yet another chance to not let them down. They are always the heroes in my mind, even though I wish none of them ever had to receive that honorary title. Through LWB, however, I continually get to work with some of the most amazing grown-ups as well, who give and give and give of themselves to help others who are hurting. Nurses, social workers, teachers, and volunteers…who get up each day wanting to make the lives of children better but who often find themselves swimming in an overwhelming ocean of pain.

In 2019, I made my first trip to India. All of us at LWB had wanted to further establish foster care there. We had been trying for over three years to find a locally run organization in India to be the right partner for family-based care. I was so happy to have connected online with Rajendra Meher, the founder and director of Youth Council for Developmental Alternatives, more commonly known as YCDA. Rajendra and his team were based in rural Odisha, one of the poorest states in India. I knew I was going to like meeting him in person, because he had already shared with me by email that he felt foster care was an essential step in strengthening India's child welfare system. He strongly believed that while children may have some of their basic needs, such as food and clothing, met in an orphanage, most do not receive the attention and love that a family can provide.

I headed to India in June of that year with my friend Arlene Howard, who had been with LWB almost since the beginning and who had successfully helped set up foster care programs in both China and Cambodia. It was one of the longest journeys overseas I had ever made, as to save money, I had routed myself on the cheapest budget airlines I could find. I drove three hours from Jacksonville to Orlando before catching a flight to Scotland and then another to Birmingham.

Arlene and I then met up to drive to London for our flight to Delhi and then on to Bhubaneswar, before finally getting in a van to make the six-hour trip across the mountains to western Odisha.

The scenery of Odisha was spectacular, as we passed through wooded hills dotted with tiny villages and houses with thatched roofs. Our driver was amazing, hitting speeds of 120 to 140 km/hour while artfully dodging the hundreds of cows we passed. I'm sure you already know that cows are generally considered sacred in India, with the highest population in the world of over 45 million cattle. They are allowed to wander anywhere they like, and so we kept passing cows walking into homes, into shops…and, amazingly, sleeping in the middle of roads, seemingly oblivious to all the traffic trying their best not to hit them. I asked the driver how bad it would be to kill a cow with your car, and he simply replied, "VERY bad indeed." We also drove past a part of the forest where wild monkeys came running out of the trees to examine our car, many holding babies, which to an animal lover like myself was pretty darn exciting.

We finally arrived at the YCDA headquarters in Boudh around noon. We were met with flowers and a beautiful chalked welcome message in front of their office. Rajendra and his team then carefully went over all the programs they were running in this severely impoverished part of India, where thousands of children live without parental care.

In order for us to better understand the legal processes involved in India when a child is relinquished or found abandoned, Rajendra had arranged for us to meet with representatives from all aspects of child protection services, including the local police and child welfare courts. Any sympathy I was feeling for myself over being jet-lagged from our long journey quickly evaporated when I saw firsthand just how hard everyone was working in this region to help at-risk children.

At the police station, one young officer walked me through the steps of what happens when a child goes missing or a baby is found on their own. In this particular rural location, files are not computerized.

Everywhere I looked there were stacks and stacks of manila folders, crammed into bookcases and piled high on desks. Each folder contained the name and case report of a vulnerable child. The young man told me that even working six days a week, from early morning until long after dark, the work was never finished. Each child protection officer was following over 250 cases during every two-week period. With the volume that this one small district does in child welfare cases, I just kept wondering about the numbers in cities like Mumbai or Kolkata.

One of the most emotional moments of our time in India was visiting a Child Welfare Committee, more commonly known as the CWC. India has a wealth of laws regarding children, and an incredibly detailed system documented on paper on how things are supposed to be handled. This includes groups made up of both unpaid positions (such as Village Child Protection Committees) and positions which are salaried by the government (such as District Protection Officers). The Child Welfare Committee serves as a child court body for each village or town, and the members of the court are unpaid volunteers. When you are elected to this court, you make a promise to work a minimum of 20 hours per week, but the court members we met said it is more like a 30 to 40 hour weekly commitment, on top of their full-time outside jobs.

The CWC is the body who decides what happens to children referred to the court under the Care and Protection of Children Act of 2015. This book of laws is hundreds of pages long, and the justices continually refer to it when making their decisions. They allowed me to skim quickly through its pages. In great detail the book describes the legal steps to take when a child is abandoned, trafficked, tortured, or forced into child marriage, all unfortunately common events in a country with over a billion people.

I was very grateful that the CWC had agreed to grant us so much time in their terribly busy schedules. We talked at length about their work and the difficulty of the cases they see. One woman on the court told us, with a defeated sense of weariness, about a newborn baby girl who had been discovered that morning when dogs were fighting over her body. The woman was required, as a representative of the CWC, to go in person to the scene to document that nothing further could be done for the child. As I listened to her tell the story, I could see the emotional toll that it takes on a person's heart to work with the volume and degree of atrocities seen each day. She quickly moved on to discuss another baby who had been admitted to a local orphanage the day before, saying, "It is wonderful that this child lived. The outcome could have been much different for a newborn, being discarded on a train platform."

Female infanticide in rural India is sadly still common, and it was very noticeable that there are far more boys than girls in the villages. When questioned, the court officers said the primary reason families do not want girls is because of the dowry system. It is just too expensive to have a daughter for many families, as you must "pay out," versus having a son who gets a "pay in" upon marriage. Because of this belief, the daughters of those who strongly consider girls a burden are sometimes killed in utero (for those who can afford ultrasounds) or abandoned or killed after birth. For this reason, the gender birth ratio in India is one of the most skewed in the world.

Boys are sometimes abandoned as well, but in those cases, it is almost always because of poverty. Many families make the decision to leave a child when they feel it is necessary to keep the other children in the family from starving. This is a sobering reality that we see in almost every country where we work.

Right at that moment in our discussions, the police brought in a 2-year-old boy who had been abandoned earlier that day. It was horrible to watch, as this beautiful little boy with huge, terrified eyes was placed in a plastic chair at the end of the table to be questioned. All I could see were his panicked black eyes, as his head barely reached the table height. The questioning by the court members began: *"Where are you from?" "Who are your parents?"* But the little boy just continued to cry. When his sobs reached a point of absolute exhaustion, he was led out to sit in the next room, of course with no answers, while the court formally declared him abandoned and gave the order for him to be taken to an orphanage. It was awful to see it unfold.

We talked later with the court members about the difficulties of questioning children who are so traumatized by what they've experienced, and they admitted it is a tough situation. They told us about a case where a child who was 6 or 7 came in completely paralyzed with fear. Despite in-depth questioning, the child wouldn't utter a sound. And so, the child went into orphanage care, where he remained completely silent. Not a single word was spoken for eight long months inside the institution. Then, finally one afternoon, he suddenly told them his name, his parents' names, and where he lived. He had actually been lost on a train, not abandoned. The trauma of being separated from his mom and taken by strangers to the court and then an orphanage had left the little boy without his voice.

Once the little boy finally found the courage to talk to the orphanage staff, he was quickly reunified with his parents, who had been searching for him the entire time. The CWC admitted that, in many regions, there is still an old and archaic system in place, where information about missing children is not passed on from one town to another. There is no national computerized system to track children who are lost. For many working in the field of child welfare and protection, this leaves them in a constant state of moral distress, wondering what more they could do to make sure each lost child finds their way home.

The immensity of their jobs is clearly a heavy burden to bear. So how do they keep going each day, despite all the sadness and trauma they are exposed to through their work? I later asked Rajendra for his thoughts.

> *In YCDA, we have been working with vulnerable children living with difficult circumstances since the beginning years of our existence. Our team's mental health is so important, as it influences how we think, feel, and behave in daily life. It also affects our ability to cope with stress, overcome challenges, build relationships, and recover from life's*

setbacks and hardships. Being mentally or emotionally healthy is much more than being free of depression, anxiety, or other psychological issues. Strong mental health refers to the presence of positive thinking and reflection as well.

Making a determined, daily effort to reflect on the positive reasons we do this work is definitely one of the ways I have coped personally with the difficult things I've experienced through LWB. There is just no escaping that by deeply loving the children in our care, there are times we must grieve deeply as well. Not every story in our work has the happy ending we so desperately desire. It is in those times of great sorrow that being able to pull up the memories of children we HAVE succeeded in helping can bring enormous solace. Positive reflection and moments of gratitude renew our resilience to keep caring for others.

When we met with the CWC that day in Odisha, I saw the same coping strategy on full display. As we all sat quietly trying to process the cries of the terrified little boy who had just been taken to the orphanage, the woman who earlier had to confirm the gruesome death of a baby suddenly reached for her phone. "Let me show you some photos of twin girls who had been abandoned to die, but who were rescued and rehabilitated for adoption." Then the whole committee pulled out their phones as well, to show us pictures of the twins in their new home, laughing and smiling with their adoptive parents. A collective breath of happiness, reminding us all why we must keep moving forward.

While resilience of individuals is something I think about continually, I am also greatly interested in the resilience of communities and cultures. I've already written about some of the traumatic history of Cambodia, with one quarter of the population losing their lives in the years of the Khmer Rouge regime. Before we began working in Uganda, I read everything I could find on the Lord's

Resistance Army and the horrific tragedies endured by children abducted as child soldiers under the leadership of Joseph Kony. How do countries recover from such monstrous abuse, especially in areas where mental health services are almost nonexistent? Through our work, I've come to believe that resilience can be taught, learned, and even handed down, as there are many communities who make a conscious decision to choose hope, even when living in the most difficult situations. Helen Keller sure got it right when she said, *"Although the world is full of suffering, it is also full of the overcoming of it."*

In 2018, I was fortunate to have three Cambodian teens from one of the rural villages where we work come and live with me for several months while they attended an intensive English language program at the University of North Florida. It was the first time I had hosted any of the kids in our programs here in the US, and it was a wonderful experience to be able to spend more than just a few hours with the students like I often only can do on my busy trips to their country.

We had a lot of fun firsts, including their first trip to a zoo to see elephants and giraffes, first time in a kayak, and first time eating Italian food (which they definitely didn't prefer). We had a lot of laughs about some of the language differences as well. For some reason they thought my use of the word "baby" to describe the baby corn and baby carrots I put in their stir fries was absolutely hysterical. But I got to laugh even harder when they asked to try "sexy dogs" one evening, which finally translated to an all-American hot dog. Yes, the word "hot" has several different meanings. They also couldn't understand why I would feed my dog Sam "burned brown balls" versus giving him the food I made each night for us to eat, since there isn't packaged dog food in their villages. They kept looking over at his food bowl saying, "Poor Sam." I know Sam was thinking the exact same thing!

Every night after dinner, we would sit at my kitchen table and discuss a topic of interest, so they could practice their English and so that I could better understand their everyday lives back home. No topic was off limits, and I sure learned a lot from our conversations about the biggest challenges they and their families were facing. I learned so much about the sobering issues that arise in the villages with severe poverty, substance abuse, and even organized crime. We also discussed the ever-present issue of trafficking along the border region where they lived.

Almost every family in their villages knew someone who had been a victim, as human trafficking is deeply interwoven with poverty. Destitute people are extremely vulnerable, as they are willing to take greater risks to find work and money to feed their families. Agreeing to travel to unfamiliar places with the lure of a paying job leaves them highly open to exploitation.

Because Southeast Asia has so much poverty, it is quite common for traffickers to prey on the youth by promising essential funds to families if they will allow their daughters to work in a distant city. The parents are told their girls will work in fancy restaurants or clean homes for wealthy clients, being able to send large amounts of money back home to support the rest of the family. It is important to remember that child labor is prevalent in the rural regions of Cambodia, and it is often expected that even young children will contribute financially to the family.

One story shared was about a recruiter who came to the village supposedly representing a restaurant in a major city which needed new waitresses. The families were told that the girls would be paid well and could live together in a dorm-style residence to save on living expenses. One of the families agreed to let their daughter go for the job after assurances that it was safe and lucrative. The labor broker said that the restaurant was so well off that it would even provide free transportation. The van showed up a few days later with a male driver, along with a female "representative of the restaurant," which put the families at ease. A few other young girls were already in the van, excited to become waitresses as well.

On the long drive to the city, the woman offered bottles of water to all the new recruits. The girl from the village soon felt drowsy after drinking the water and fell asleep, not realizing that the woman had drugged the drinks as part of the trafficking operation. When the girl woke up, she was in a small, bare room with bars on the windows and a locked door. The only piece of furniture in the room was a bed. She was terrified when she realized that rather than a restaurant, she had been taken instead to a secret brothel.

When the locked door opened, the owner of the facility came in and told her she was now his property. When she began crying and tried to resist, he raped and beat her, making it clear it would happen again until she complied. Terrified and injured, she finally gave in. After several months of being forced to work as a prostitute, one of her repeat customers finally listened to her impassioned pleas for help. He agreed to assist in her escape and get her to the police. She eventually arrived back to her village broken with despair.

Another upsetting story they shared one evening happened during the time they were living with me. They had learned from their friends back home that a young man had been arrested for raping a 15-year-old girl multiple times. When I asked what would happen to him, they explained that the man would go and speak with the girl's parents. If a marriage could be arranged, the man would not be charged with a crime.

I kept saying, "But she can't be made to marry her rapist," and they kept insisting, "This is the only way to prevent shame in the family." If the families couldn't reach an agreement on marriage, then the man would serve five years in prison. I was hoping the girl's parents would not agree, although I knew with my Western way of thinking I couldn't fully understand what the girl would face culturally if she didn't marry the man who had "defiled" her. The important thing that the teens wanted me to understand, however, was that the girl had no choice but to move on. They lived in a country that had suffered through so much sorrow and grief during the brutal civil war. The message they had all been taught growing up was that whenever bad things happen, it's essential to switch your thoughts to building a good future instead. Each of them fully believed that nothing positive could come from dwelling on a painful past.

It reminded me of a conversation I had with Dr. Erik Laursen, from the University of Richmond, who developed special treatment programs for children who have lived through trauma. We had met together to discuss LWB's foster care program in Cambodia and how we could best meet the needs of village children who live where there are no licensed psychologists. Despite limited professional resources, we wanted to do everything in our power to make sure each child could heal emotionally.

Dr. Laursen spoke very eloquently about Holocaust survivors, saying that the majority of those who lived through the atrocities of the concentration camps most likely didn't receive weekly counseling sessions afterwards, as formally scheduled talk therapy is actually a very American thought process. Those who survived the horrors of the Holocaust have shown us that there IS life after trauma and that it IS possible to somehow find the strength to go on. He gave me particularly important advice that in every location where we have programs, we must strike that balance between respecting the local ways of moving forward after hardship versus interjecting a foreign belief system of how children "should feel" after living through something difficult.

I had arranged the meeting with Dr. Laursen shortly after we began our Safe Haven Foster Care program in Cambodia, which is one of the most difficult projects we run from an emotional standpoint. Our Safe Haven program was created to help children who have been trafficked or severely abused...experiences no child should ever have to endure. I am not going to share their stories. You don't need me to tell you all the absolutely evil things that an adult can do to a young child. I used to think I wanted to know, to better understand what the children in our care had experienced, but now I wish I didn't. One of our team members shared with me the overwhelming feeling of anguish she felt one day sitting with a group of children in our programs, when the chilling realization washed over her that half of the little girls innocently coloring with crayons in front of her had been violently assaulted. Wading into a world of childhood grief and trauma without expecting it to impact your own mental health is like thinking you can wade into a lake without ever getting wet. It simply isn't possible.

Working in the field of anti-trafficking is an extremely complex endeavor. I'm so grateful that Dr. Robert Spires is a member of our board of directors, since anti-trafficking is a subject he specializes in... although he'd be the first to explain that since it crosses economics, politics, sociology, criminology, and a host of other areas, you can't really label trafficking as a single field of study. Dr. Spires writes,

> *To further complicate things, human trafficking is virtually impossible to quantify due to its very nature of being a hidden practice. Several scholars and government agencies have attempted to put a specific number on human trafficking, and these numbers are not particularly trustworthy. I have seen numbers ranging from 5 million to 40 million victims of human trafficking worldwide, and even the best methodologies of estimation have fairly wide ranges of numbers. What we know, though, is that there is a lot of money to be made by trafficking people, no matter what form it takes. We also know that human trafficking cannot be addressed unless we attack it at every level, which includes the economic reality of large numbers of extremely impoverished and disadvantaged people around the world. We cannot do this without profound changes of hearts and minds across the globe.*

Love Without Boundaries had decided in 2017 that our role in attacking this problem was to provide a safe and secure place where children who had been trafficked or abused could heal: in a family setting. Usually, children rescued from these situations are placed into shelters, but we believed that healing could be found in individual homes instead. When the program launched in Cambodia, it quickly filled with children, ranging in age from babies to pre-teens, who had lived through the unthinkable.

As I mentioned, however, one of the first issues we faced is that psychologists and counselors are very rare in Cambodia. The few in practice are all located far from the rural region where we are working. To help treat the children not only physically but emotionally, we knew that we would need to begin training local staff and social workers on the ground. In September of that year, we sent a team of trauma specialists to Cambodia to do full assessments and create care plans for the children in our foster care program who had been victims of violence.

A few weeks later, we were asked to take in three additional children to our Safe Haven program. As I was being told about the last child, I found myself pressing my nails as hard as I could into the palm of my hand to try and stop myself from crying. The youngest child's injuries were so severe they required hospitalization, and this precious little one, of course, was completely traumatized and shut down. I hung up the phone and sat in silence for a long time before getting on a call with our team to discuss what our first steps needed to be to begin her journey of healing.

What I have learned over the years is that there is no set of instructions that tell you how to overcome trauma, grief, and pain. There is no way to say, "Just do A, then B and C, and all will be well." There isn't even a finish line in most cases. You might think you have won the battle when suddenly another memory or wave comes crashing down in a child's life to show that the finish line you were hoping to have crossed has been moved even further down field.

But we will never give up trying, asking people who are highly trained and who have more experience than ourselves what more we can be doing. I believe that 90% of the healing process for the children in this special foster care program is just getting them to truly feel safe. Making sure they have food, clothing, access to school…these are things that help build security. A feeling of safety is the most important thing we can provide, especially when given by foster parents who care. As a team, we continually work toward our major goal of helping each child who has been wounded learn to love well, and thus live well. This is our continued prayer.

In speaking with trauma experts like Dr. Laursen, I also respect that not every child who goes through something unthinkable will have lifelong effects. We should never insinuate to children that they ought to be feeling bad or like a victim because of what they have gone through, as some kids will be able to handle it on their own terms. Dr. Laursen helped free us from the guilt over not being able to provide weekly therapy with a licensed psychologist for the kids, as he believes support should often take an invitational approach instead. *"I am here to talk if you ever want someone to listen,"* or, *"You can always come share with me when you feel the time is right."* That often goes further than a scheduled therapy session every Tuesday afternoon.

He shared with me the story of a child in his care who had suffered through enormous trauma, without giving any details. The staff at the counseling center kept saying they should force her to "do her work in healing," but he insisted that it was completely up to the girl when she would feel ready. She left the center after a year without ever confiding in anyone. About 15 years later, she came into his office and said, "I want to thank you for allowing me to know when the time was right for me to open up about my experiences." She said that it wasn't until the birth of her first child that she was ready to speak to someone about her past trauma, and she was very grateful that he allowed her to come to it in her own time.

I also think it's important to remember that a child doesn't have to have a full cathartic experience to heal…a moment where they completely break down so they can be built back up. Healing is often a lifelong process, and there isn't anything wrong with that. Our role with our Safe Haven program is to make sure the children know there are caring people to whom they can talk, without judgement, whenever they choose.

Because trauma is stored in the body in so many different ways, we look at each child in foster care and work with them on their own to decide where they "find calmness." For some, it is through art. For others, it may be through exercise, like swimming or playing soccer. Some children in our Safe Haven program love music, while others have found peace through the joy of raising puppies. Each of them hears the message, *"You are strong... You can get through this... We believe in you."* As they grow, we want them to know they are survivors, but, of course, for every one of them I pray they move beyond just surviving to actually embracing life.

When I think of the children who have been so deeply harmed by adults, whether through institutional care, severe abuse at home, or from a crime like trafficking, I know absolutely that evil exists in our world. I have seen it far too many times. But I've also come to realize that when you've faced evil...looked right at its core...then you are able to better understand what goodness truly means. So many times, goodness isn't some grand thing with bright lights and lavish gestures. It's often small and unassuming. Goodness is tender, like holding someone's hand in solace or really listening without feeling a need to speak. It comes in bedtime stories, cooking a child's favorite meal, or gently combing their hair. Sincere goodness lets a child breathe in hope.

Dr. Taiki Matsuura, from Yale University, once wrote: *"Despite all of the talk about resilience being an individual trait, most of us are only as resilient as we are loved."* I think that sums it up perfectly, and it's why we work so hard to make sure the children who need us come to feel how much they are valued. Our world...while often beautiful and bright...is also filled with suffering. I don't believe anyone can escape pain, although I'll never understand why some children are given such an uneven share.

I recently gave each of my children a copy of Charlie Mackesy's beautiful book *The Boy, The Mole, The Fox, and The Horse*. If you haven't read it, I would encourage you to do so. On almost every page, Mackesy had somehow found the exact words I wished each child in our programs could store deeply inside their hearts. There was one page, however, that moved me to tears as I thought of the children in our programs who have endured far too much. Above his hand-drawn image of a little boy riding a horse, he had written three perfect lines for any child of trauma:

"Sometimes," said the horse.

"Sometimes what?" asked the boy.

"Sometimes just getting up and carrying on is brave and magnificent."

And to that I can only respond, "Amen."

The Heart of Community

Chapter 10: Hope

Hope is among the most wonderful gifts we have. It keeps us going when we want to quit and makes victory possible when we thought it was absolutely unattainable. Hope is what I see in the eyes of the children in LWB programs I so closely work with. They dream to grow up into beautiful human beings and make a difference to this world. For them, hope is not wishful thinking. Hope is an emotion, a mindset, a belief, a motivation, that despite setbacks and obstacles, despite hardship and misfortune, despite the prior chapters of their life's story, they believe that a better future lies ahead.

Suhita Biswas, LWB-India Program Manager

    As I come to this last topic of our second LWB book, of course I am going to end with what I believe is one of the most essential traits of any supportive community. I have always tried to live my life as a "glass half full" kind of person, as I think that, when life completely pours rain down upon your shoulders, trying to search for even the smallest glimmer of hope is essential to keep moving forward. The reality, though, is that even the most ardent optimists have times when their cups run completely dry…when they can't possibly take another disappointment or sorrow. No one can escape pain in this life, but it is during these moments that being part of a caring and authentic community can be truly life changing. These are the moments when the sisterhoods and brotherhoods we've formed along the way can give us the encouragement and strength to keep going.

Since the word "hope" is used repeatedly by charities all over the world, it is something I have definitely reflected upon. The number of quotes about hope that you can find online has to be one of the largest collections out there, but what IS hope exactly? What does it mean to you personally when you pull up that word in your mind? I'd like to share three final stories which have shown me yet again why the age-old adage to never lose hope has been passed down by countless generations.

Earlier in this book, I wrote about our emergency food relief efforts to help families greatly impacted by the pandemic. One evening, after an exceptionally long day of food deliveries, one of the LWB tuk-tuk drivers saw an elderly man in a field attempting to make charcoal. This process in Cambodia is a physically draining one. It involves gathering heavy rocks and stones to build a large circle for the fire mound. Then trees and brush are cut down, split into quarters, and stacked as tightly as possible inside the stone circle. The wood is covered with a dense layer of sticks and leaves, followed by a giant mound of dirt to create an almost air-tight oven. It is then slowly burned for days, under constant supervision, to make sure it only smolders. Anything more would reduce the wood to a useless ash.

The driver could see that the grandfather in the field was struggling with such an arduous task, and so he quickly pulled over to see if he could help. It was then that he realized that Grandpa Mung was living outdoors with his six small grandchildren and elderly wife. The youngest of the children were 3-year-old twins, and the oldest was just 9. The children's parents had abandoned them, leaving the aging grandparents in a desperate situation. Grandpa Mung's wife had become seriously ill the year before, and selling their small home and plot of land was the only way they could afford her medical care. Now homeless, Grandpa Mung's only choice at that point was to tie several blue tarps to a few cut-down tree limbs to try and protect the children and his wife from the monsoonal rains.

Despite having this makeshift shelter, things had remained extremely difficult. The entire family was grateful that LWB was able to provide them with emergency food supplies for the month. Although Grandpa Mung told our team that he was not normally comfortable accepting charity, the well-being of his grandchildren was paramount.

In talking with the family, we learned that Grandpa Mung, like countless others in Cambodia, had been impacted deeply by the civil war. He had grown up with seven brothers and sisters, as the youngest child in a large and loving family. Then came the declaration by the Khmer Rouge that 1975 would officially become Year Zero, to signify the rebirth of Cambodian history. Schools and hospitals were closed, books and money were banned, and hundreds of thousands of people were forced into agricultural labor camps where they were overworked and starved. Family relationships not sanctioned by the new government were forbidden, and husbands, wives, and children were often separated by force. Family members who tried to communicate with one another could even be executed.

In Year Zero, Mr. Mung was taken from his parents and forced to join the army. He and countless others quickly learned one of the Khmer Rouge's mottos that "To keep you is no benefit. To destroy you is no loss." It was a time of pure survival. Grandpa Mung said that all during the war he never received one piece of news about his parents or other siblings. After the war ended in 1979, he returned home to his village, longing to see his family once again. When he got to their old house, however, he found it completely empty.

He asked the remaining villagers where his family had gone, and they solemnly said that Angka had come and invited his family to a training. Angka, which translates to "the organization" in the Khmer language, was one of the most feared words of the war. Surprisingly, very few Cambodians even knew at the beginning of the war which individual leaders were actually running the country, as the heads of the Khmer Rouge believed that complete secrecy was one of the most powerful tools they had to control the public. Instead, people were simply told that Angka was now in charge and that Angka had complete power. It was common for Angka troops to come into a village and provide forced "training" on the country's new ideologies, which sadly was just a tactic to take people away for execution.

Grandpa Mung thought that his entire family most likely had been killed, but he lived in the run-down village home for over a year, waiting and hoping for his siblings to come back. He knew that his close-knit family would have moved heaven and earth to return home to each other, so he waited patiently for any of them to once again come through the door. No one ever arrived. He finally had to accept the harsh reality that his entire family had perished during the war. With everyone he loved now gone, he decided to leave his village, traveling from one area to another with the purpose of helping others. A few years later, he met Grandma Mung, and love finally returned to his life.

Together, this quiet couple lived a life of subsistence, working for decades on construction sites doing backbreaking work and receiving wages that barely covered food. Wanting so much to have a better future, when a trafficking broker promised them good jobs in Thailand doing construction, they crossed the border, dreaming of finally being able to escape poverty. Instead, they were held captive on various sites for eight years, with an extremely abusive boss. When a construction site where they were working was raided one day, they and the other migrants were arrested. After spending time in a Thai jail, they were finally released and allowed to make their way back home to Cambodia. Now, over 40 years later, they found themselves once again with no home and no income, this time trying to raise six young grandchildren.

This devoted couple worked so hard to care for their grandchildren, whom they dearly loved. After having to sell their house to save the life of his wife, Grandpa Mung had come up with the idea to make charcoal in an attempt to feed his family. It was a grueling task, evidenced by his hands which were deeply cut and burned from the process. As our driver looked around at the mounds of charcoal which had already been processed, an idea quickly came to him. He explained to Grandpa Mung that LWB has several "kitchen houses" at our primary schools. The cooks need fuel every day to prepare hot lunches for the students. Why couldn't LWB purchase the grandfather's charcoal for our schools so he could earn some needed income for his family? A mutual agreement was quickly sealed.

Grandpa Mung then showed the driver how he was trying to plant a garden to provide his wife and children with food. He had taken a large tree branch and tied two watering cans to each end with some twine. He would walk the long way to a nearby pond to fill the watering cans, and then carry them back on his thin, stooped shoulders to give water to the seedlings. It was a process he had to repeat many times each day to keep the tiny plants fed.

The LWB driver was deeply moved by the gentle kindness of the grandfather, who was giving everything he had to make sure his family was cared for. He called our director Leng to let him know about this at-risk family, and together they came up with a plan. Our team decided to provide Grandpa Mung with a small water pump and irrigation hoses, which could quickly transfer the water from the pond. They also returned with additional vegetable seeds to add to his small crop.

These dedicated grandparents are incredibly hard workers. They cleared the field and immediately started planting and tending the garden carefully. Each time our team returned, they could see the results of the family's labors. The plants in the fields thrived, and, within just a few months, Grandpa and Grandma Mung were able to begin selling vegetables to our school lunch program and to a local market as well. They now make enough funds each week to provide food for the entire family.

When we asked whether the children were receiving an education, we learned that they lived too far from the government school to get there by walking. One of the things that weighs on my heart is just how many children around the world are not receiving any education whatsoever, because of just a small amount of needed funding. In so many regions where we work, even in places where there are free government schools, there are children who do not attend because they lack something as basic as school supplies or a required uniform. Or in this case...a simple child's bike.

Cue up another special delivery, as two bicycles were quickly purchased for the Mungs' grandchildren, allowing the oldest four to ride tandem to the nearest government school. Leng went with the children on their first day to help them enroll, and it took no time at all for them to be introduced to their classmates and begin making new friends.

The Mungs' story does not stop there. When one of our wonderful supporters heard this large family was living outside in a field, a donation was received to build a small home for them as well. Nothing too fancy – just a simple metal structure since Grandpa Mung wants to earn his own way – but enough that the children now have a safe, dry home to call their very own.

When we spoke with Grandpa Mung one weekend, surrounded by his thriving plants, we asked how he had kept going. After facing so many difficult struggles throughout his life, including the loss of his land and home as a senior citizen, what helps him keep moving forward? He thought for a moment and then began speaking about his grandchildren. Grandpa Mung explained that he and his wife had never received an education. Neither was able to read or write, making it impossible to open the pages of a book to learn more about our world. "I carry the hope that my grandchildren will have a life that doesn't look like ours," he said with a quiet resolve. "My grandchildren will be educated people. They will all finish high school and be able to create their own futures. Even though my dreams for my own life have always failed, I will never stop working for theirs to come true. Just as we tend a garden, we must tend hope as well."

I know that our team in Cambodia had been so concerned for this family's well-being since they first came upon them under a meager tarp in an empty field. Those worries then turned to a sense of peace after seeing the hard work and determination of the grandparents produce a bountiful harvest. At LWB, we love celebrating new beginnings…no matter one's age. Grandpa Mung and his wife remind us that hope is far more than just magically wishing things would get better. Hope is holding onto the belief that our lives CAN improve, and then taking the steps to help put it to action.

———————

When LWB's work first began on the mainland of China, the orphanages I would visit looked remarkably similar in their populations, with row after row of baby cribs filled with "healthy" baby girls. This is the image of Chinese orphanages many people still mistakenly hold in their minds today. The primary reason so many baby girls were originally there was because families in China were subject to the One Child policy, and the cultural preference was for sons. Female infant abandonment was known and fairly common, and so almost every baby I would be handed was a girl. This was reflected in international adoptions as well, as 95% of the children finding homes in the international program from 1991 to 2006 were girls with no special needs.

With each passing year, however, the percentage of children in China being born with birth defects began to rise exponentially. Data in 2018 showed that over one million children a year were being born in China with medical needs. The most common birth defects reported were congenital heart disease, missing limbs, cleft lip and palate, and neural tube defects, but the special needs ranged from mild to severe and affected every body system.

With this increased rate of birth defects came a rise in the abandonment of children with medical needs, primarily for two reasons. Either the cost of providing medical care to the child was simply too high for an impoverished family to afford, or the family was unable to accept the often-enormous stigmas surrounding children with disabilities. By the time the One Child policy was finally repealed on October 29, 2015, almost every child being abandoned in China had some sort of special need.

When we would share the stories of orphaned children who had been left on their own with medical conditions such as cleft, cerebral palsy, or often complex heart defects, I would frequently have people tell me how terrible they thought it was that anyone would abandon a child who was sick. I see similar comments on social media in both China and the West with regular frequency. I remember having a discussion at an adoption conference with a parent who told me quite frankly that she would never honor her daughter's birth parents because they had "thrown her away" when she was born needing surgery.

Through working in China since 2003, I have learned that child abandonment is a complex subject that cannot be summed up in simple black or white statements. There are just so many reasons why children end up in orphanage care. I remember being in a children's hospital on one of my trips and having a father approach our director in China with his 1-year-old son in his arms. The man who stood in front of us looked decades older than his true age. His face was heavily lined and wind chapped from working outside all day. He wore a threadbare coat and shoes which had almost lost their soles. He asked if we were part of the group who helped provide free surgeries to orphaned children. When our director confirmed that we were, he quietly began to tell us that his son was dying of a complex heart defect but that his family had no possible means of raising the money needed to save his life. The father had tried earning extra funds by fixing bicycle tires in his village, but he was still making just $2 to $3 a day. Simply feeding his family was a constant worry. Finding the funds for a $10,000 surgery was beyond impossible.

The man told us that he and his wife had tried to borrow from people in their village, but everyone knew that they would never be repaid, and so he had only raised $320. He said it would take him at least a year to pay that sum back. He had taken a long bus ride to Shanghai with his son with the hope that a hospital in such a wealthy city would provide his child's needed surgery and allow him to pay the bill slowly over time. He was told, however, that without having the funds up front, there could be no operation.

Later, I learned that he quietly asked our Chinese director the next morning if we would consider helping his son if he gave his child to us permanently. He had heard rumors in the hospital hallways that we were providing free medical care to orphaned children. The heart hospital in Shanghai was often a last chance attempt for rural families, who showed up in desperation when other hospitals in their province had turned them away. You can imagine how difficult it was for these families to hear that orphaned children could receive free surgeries through several different NGOs, while their own children who were sick were turned away. The father told our director that if it meant his little boy would have a chance to live, then he would leave him to our care. He wasn't "throwing his son away" by offering the child to our team. He was willing to make the ultimate sacrifice if it meant the child he loved could finally get his life-saving heart surgery.

I remember sitting in my hotel room that night wondering what it would be like to know that your child was dying, while also knowing that no medical assistance would be given without payment up front. I honestly couldn't think about it for too long, because it just made me so sad to think about how many families around the world feel that desperation every day. Thankfully, for this family, we were able to arrange for heart surgery for the little boy through our Unity Initiative. I was blessed to be able to meet the little boy and his dad the next year when I visited their province. I will never forget their smiles and how the father appeared to be ten years younger now that the weight of not being able to help his sick child had been removed from his shoulders. The little boy was now an energetic toddler, who was obviously aware that he was completely cherished. The pride and love for his little boy was unmistakable on his father's face.

Our Unity Initiative program is very dear to my heart, as I can't help but wonder how many children who ended up in orphanage care could have remained with their families if extra encouragement and medical support could have been provided from the very beginning. I am grateful that the LWB community has rallied behind this important program, and I'm also thankful that the government of China continues to put additional funding into its rural insurance programs.

As I mentioned, there is another reason why so many children with medical needs end up in orphanage care as well – the huge social stigma which still exists in China today for many children born with birth defects. Especially in the rural regions of the country, giving birth to a child with special needs is actually viewed as a moral failing on the part of the parents, bringing shame to the entire family.

In the last few years, however, the number of children entering Chinese orphanages with birth defects which can be diagnosed by ultrasound has fallen dramatically. In May 2021, it was announced that there had been a 30% drop in the number of children residing in government orphanages compared to 2019. The government's new Zero Birth Defects Plan calls for a greater awareness of eugenics and aims "to harness the power of technology, society, and families to actively promote tertiary prevention measures to prevent birth defects and improve the quality of society." With ultrasounds being done in even the most remote regions of China now, many babies in utero who have issues like missing limbs, cleft, or heart defects are no longer being born. This, of course, is difficult for me to dwell deeply upon, particularly as the mom to a child who is missing his right forearm. We've seen firsthand in so many orphanages that most children now entering institutional care have medical needs which cannot be easily diagnosed by ultrasound before delivery. We hear from other organizations as well that they are seeing similar trends. For example, one charity we have worked with on cleft surgeries has told us that, in the last few years, there are far fewer babies with cleft lip in the regions where they serve. Under the Zero Birth Defects Plan, many are no longer being born.

What it has meant for our own work with orphaned children is that so many of the wonderful kids now being referred to LWB have multiple, complex needs…needs which require true one-on-one attention for a child to make as much progress as possible. That usually can't happen in the typical orphanage setting, and I think regularly about how much is completely lost when a child born with medical needs is raised without a family.

One of the children in our healing home in 2021, for example, is a 3-year-old little girl named Nora. She is an absolutely beautiful child, with the sweetest little smile and a full head of black hair that she loves having up in a messy bun or pigtails. She came into our care a few months after her first birthday, weighing only 11 pounds. Nora was severely delayed in her orphanage, unable to hold up her head or even roll side to side. Our nannies described her as floppy, and the local doctor had given her a very nonspecific "brain maldevelopment" diagnosis.

After just one week of being in our healing home, Nora revealed that, with lots of love and daily encouragement, she was a child ready to blossom. She began clinging like a little monkey to her nanny, as she craved being held after lying in an orphanage crib for over a year and staring at a blank ceiling. Soon she was smiling and even holding toys. Just three months after leaving her orphanage, she was already saying "mama" and enthusiastically throwing open her arms wanting to snuggle.

Just before her second birthday, Nora gained the strength needed to sit up by herself and was putting words together to let her needs be known. She discovered a love for cartoons and having her hair fixed with colorful bows. Right as she turned 3, she went from standing nervously on her own to suddenly walking around her bed while holding onto the sides. She loves when her nanny plays chase with her, and she will scoot as fast as she can around the bed while giggling loudly. When her nanny catches her, Nora will put her head down on the bed sheet as if to hide and then start the game all over again. I am certain she will soon be walking independently and then moving onto running. Nora is a child with her own unique timeline, which we respect completely.

What hurts my heart is that I've sadly seen, too many times, what life is often like for other little "Noras" when they are confined to institutional care. When they spend their days lying flat on their backs. When they are rarely hugged or even touched with affection. When children with special needs are denied their right to a caring home. I've seen gauntness and pressure sores and atrophy and succumbing.

The pandemic changed so many aspects of life all around the world, didn't it? Another area impacted by the virus is adoption. I know that international adoption has become an extremely controversial topic now, with some groups calling for its complete abolishment. I do not agree with closing the program completely. Our charity has always been a vocal proponent of only allowing fully ethical adoptions. Back in 2008, when it became clear that China's domestic adoption numbers were rising rapidly, LWB was one of the first charities to publicly state that international adoptions of "healthy" children from China were no longer needed, as those children could now be chosen by local families and grow up in the country of their birth. That remains our hope for every single child who is orphaned…that a family in their own community or culture would want to give them a permanent home. In 2021, however, there are still thousands of children in Chinese orphanages who will not be chosen by local families. Their special needs still carry too much stigma or shame. Sadly, Nora is one such child.

The positive news is that most people working in this field (myself included) believe the current hesitancy to adopt children born with disabilities will continue to change. That is a hope to hold onto tightly. I look back at America's history concerning special needs, for example, and we've thankfully seen such a powerful shift in the last few decades. It is difficult to think that around the same time I was born in the 1960s, our country was still locking children with Down syndrome inside state institutions, depriving them of family care. It was also common practice for life-saving surgeries to be withheld from children born with disabilities. As late as the 1980s, in a case that went to the Supreme Court of Indiana, a baby with Down syndrome was denied surgery for esophageal atresia, which had a high surgical success rate. Multiple families stepped forward offering to adopt the baby when they learned she was being denied food and water, but their urgent pleas were all refused. The little girl passed away just one week later. Thanks to an enormous public outcry, Congress passed an amendment to the national Child Abuse Law a few years later to protect newborns with special needs. Just as America continues to evolve in our care and protection of children born with disabilities, I know other countries will make similar progress as well.

For now, however, there are children with special needs all over the world who are being deprived of permanent homes. While I truly wish every child could grow up in the country of their birth, if there is a choice between being confined to an institution 24/7 versus having a family say, "We would love to welcome this child, regardless of their needs, as our own son or daughter," I'll argue for the latter until the very end. I've seen too much hurt and too much suffering to not believe children with medical needs deserve families, regardless of geographical and political borders.

Through adoption, I have seen so many children born with special needs be given the ability to absolutely shine. I cheer in front of my computer when I get messages about children formerly in LWB programs now winning medals in sporting events or graduating from high school. They're in dance classes and taking art lessons and attending Sunday school and play groups. They're reading Braille and getting their first jobs. They are loved by their adoptive families, all throughout the world, and cherished in the way that EVERY child deserves.

Whenever I get discouraged in this work, I try to close my eyes, take a deep breath, and pull up the faces of children in whose lives, even for a short time, we were allowed to take part. With her mom's permission, I would like to share the story of Emily. Whenever I need a bit of hope to hold onto, Emily's beautiful face is one which frequently comes to mind.

I first met Emily while visiting an orphanage in southern China. She was lying flat on her back in an old metal crib, with a blanket covering her body. She was incredibly tiny. As I drew closer, the nanny uncovered the baby to show me that Emily had been born with not only a cleft lip but also missing one of her arms and both of her legs just below her hips. Honestly, the very first thought that immediately came to my mind was, "She has got to get out of here in order to survive." When we asked the orphanage director whether they had decided to file Emily's adoption paperwork, I was thrilled to learn that her file had already been sent to the national government. No one had come forward yet, though, to choose Emily as their daughter.

Thankfully, LWB had a cleft surgery team coming to China the very next month. We immediately began working on the logistics of having Emily travel from Guangdong Province up to Henan so that her cleft lip could be repaired. During her pre-op tests with our medical team, however, it was discovered that Emily had another special need that would make her lip surgery more difficult: an undiagnosed heart defect. Usually on our cleft trips, when a child is found to have any sort of heart condition, we do not move forward with the lip operation until after we can arrange for the heart defect to be healed first. Since Emily had such a variety of extra conditions, though, the pediatric anesthesiologist on our team made the decision to move ahead with surgery in the hope that her ability to eat and gain weight could then improve.

We were so happy that Emily's lip repair went smoothly, despite her cardiac issues. The trip volunteers all agreed it was impossible not to fall in love with this petite, sweet girl. She liked to be propped up on her hospital bed in a sitting position so she could quietly observe everything happening on the ward. She also loved having people stop by to smile and speak to her, reaching out her hand to grab onto their finger or an offered toy.

We were concerned about sending Emily back to an orphanage after learning that she had a sizable hole between the upper chambers of her heart, so we requested permission to move her to our Heartbridge Healing Home. Thankfully, her orphanage agreed to the transfer. The nannies at Heartbridge worked diligently to improve Emily's health, in preparation for her open-heart surgery which we had scheduled in three months' time.

Emily continued to show everyone that she had a colossal inner strength, as this pint-sized girl sailed through her cardiac surgery in Shanghai as well. Following her operation, Emily's energy level increased dramatically. Her nannies in the healing home loved describing her as an extremely sweet but strong-willed little princess. She loved to be cuddled and wasn't about to let her missing limbs slow her down in any way. When she wanted to reach a toy or her nanny, she would simply roll across the floor...and she didn't want any help doing so, thank you very much!

At around the same time as her surgery, a family in the US saw Emily's photo and requested to view her adoption file. It is fairly standard practice that when a family is given an adoption file to consider, they will send the file to medical experts to get their opinions on a child's particular needs. The family looking at Emily's file sent it to four separate physicians, and all four doctors told the family they should NOT move forward to bring her home. They said Emily would never move, never talk, and that she would essentially be a "vegetable" (their awful word, not mine).

The mom in the US just kept looking at Emily's little face, however, and she made a request to the orphanage for a video clip of the baby, which showed her interacting with a nanny. One physician who viewed the video said Emily's reactions were no different than those of Pavlov's dogs, and I smiled when the mom said she was ready to climb through the telephone wire to throttle the doctor. She told me later that she could see the determination in Emily's eyes, even if the doctors couldn't. "*We knew God had planted her deep in our hearts and decided that if she had been born to us, we would have done everything possible to give her the best life. God knew...and I'm so glad we listened."*

Just one year after her adoption, Emily's mom shared an update with us on her beautiful daughter:

This little girl amazes me every day. She is so strong, both physically and in her will. She has started speech therapy and is making lots of sounds. Every now and then, she pops up with a very clear word that she is repeating. We are so thankful for LWB and the Cleft Exchange for repairing her lip at a young age, so these sounds are so much easier for her to make. One of these days she'll be talking a mile a minute, and we are sure looking forward to that. She definitely gets her point across by using gestures, and she is even starting to use some sign language, though some signs are difficult for her since so many signs require two hands.

We took her to see a cardiologist here, just to make sure everything looked good. The ultrasound tech stopped over the repaired part of her heart. I was starting to wonder what he was looking at when he said, 'That's amazing!' The surgeon she saw also commented on the excellent repair she received on her heart in Shanghai.

Emily went for her second fitting for her double leg prostheses recently. They measured, cut, drilled, etc. and were about ready to call it quits for the day when I asked her if she wanted to try and walk. I supported her under her arms and away she went. They asked if I would walk in front of her to see if she would walk toward me while they held her, so they could see how she moved. At the doorway to the room, I stopped and then she stopped. They then let go and... SHE STOOD THERE UNASSISTED for about three seconds! Yes, this mama cried! The lady doing the measurements had tears in her eyes and said, 'I think we got it! This girl is going to go places!' She never ceases to amaze us.

Fast forward five more years, and I would like to find all four of those original doctors who said Emily should be institutionalized for the rest of her life. Her mom recently sent me an update that I think each one of those physicians should keep tacked up on their whiteboards, as a reminder that EVERY child has infinite worth and undiscovered possibilities:

> *Emily got a new bike at the beginning of the summer and likes to ride it around the neighborhood. She doesn't let her missing limbs slow her down! She enjoys playing games with her brothers, hopping on the trampoline, and swimming. She is playing the piano quite well. She's astonishing people that she can play with her stub. She has also gotten to be quite the artist. She enjoys drawing, coloring, and painting. She enjoys helping in the kitchen and baking, especially cake decorating. She's just finishing 4th grade (Oh, where did my baby go?). She's still a snuggle bug and an encourager to everyone. She's a pretty typical 10-year-old who likes to have her hair braided in different ways and enjoys being a fashionista. She IS amazing and makes this mama's heart very full. Thank you to everyone at LWB for taking such good care of her when she was in China waiting for us to find her.*

Whenever I think of Emily, it's impossible to not feel a sense of hope ignite again in my heart. Hope gives us strength and the belief that, if we refuse to give up, better things lie ahead. Emily went from lying in an orphanage crib to running on her prosthetic legs, adorned with silver sparkly shoes. Her remarkable progress was not only due to her own determination and grit but also because she had parents who adored her. Parents who would move mountains for her. It's what every child deserves.

As of the spring of 2020, however, all international adoptions from China were halted due to COVID. This has left so many children matched with families in an awful limbo state. In our care right now, we have an amazing little girl who is paralyzed from the waist down and whose kidney function has begun to decline. We have another girl with severe glaucoma which has left her blind, who came from a facility where she lay prone on her back. There are little boys with Down syndrome and the sweetest girl with cerebral palsy. Children who came into our care shut down and delayed, and yet each of them has such incredible potential and a deep, inherent need to feel loved. All of the children in our healing home deserve a family of their very own, just like Emily did, and our team can't imagine them not having a way out through adoption. I wrote earlier in this chapter about little Nora and the remarkable progress she is making while with us. It's extremely difficult to think of her having to return to institutional care someday, without being matched to her own mom or dad.

This is why we cling to hope, as we love the kids who come into our hands so dearly. It is why we'll never give up believing that SOMEDAY each of the children in our care will have a chance at a permanent home. Yes, we know that many orphanages have stopped filing the paperwork for children to be adopted, often citing a decline in international cooperation. Yes, we understand that all travel at the moment has been halted due to COVID concerns. I also fully realize I have absolutely zero say on any country's adoption laws and regulations. But I also know that orphanage directors retire. Public awareness of special needs adoption grows. And families in so many countries around the world are opening their hearts to children born with different abilities.

What I love about LWB is that we always err on the side of hope. We will never stop advocating for all the orphaned children in our programs to have a chance at having caring families of their own. I know there's a family out there who would count themselves completely blessed if they could wake up to Nora's sweet smiles. Who would love to read her bedtime stories and be the recipient of her gentle hugs. Even though she might not have the opportunity to be chosen for adoption at this particular moment of time, hope keeps me praying that one day…perhaps tomorrow…love will somehow find a way.

In February 2020, right before the pandemic began to change life as we knew it, a little boy came into the world in Uganda. He was a tiny little one, weighing just over four pounds, and originally the local doctors didn't see anything of worry except that the baby was small. Over the next few weeks, however, baby Izzy did not put on weight, despite breastfeeding well. His worried mom decided to find a different doctor to examine her precious son, and soon they were sent to the Uganda Heart Institute for Izzy's first echocardiogram.

It was on that visit that his parents learned Izzy had been born with Down syndrome, as well as a complete AV Canal Defect. With this cardiac defect, babies are born with a huge hole in the very center of their heart, which impacts all four chambers. In a normal heart, the right side pumps blood to the lungs while the left pumps blood to the body. For baby Izzy, the large hole in his heart allowed extra blood to enter his lung arteries, raising the pulmonary pressure and making his heart and lungs work harder. The doctor explained that without a complex surgery while he was still a baby, he would soon become inoperable, and his heart would fail.

His mom Susan told our team:

No amount of words can ever explain the turmoil we felt in our hearts at that time. It was such a time of pain. I personally kept looking at the cardiologist to try and explain this to us. I was in shock; so I didn't show any emotions at all. He must have wondered why I was being so strong, but in reality I wasn't strong. The news hit me so terribly that I couldn't think or sensibly talk to anyone. That's why I just went silent and kept looking at the cardiologist. When we reached home, I cried so terribly day and night. Where were we going to get the money for the surgery? Why had the Lord let such a thing happen to our son, our first-born child? I felt sorry for us. I felt sorry for our son. I wondered how he was feeling inside being in this state. We were filled with sorrow.

The day after the diagnosis, my husband and I went to see our pastor. We thought that maybe with prayer the Lord would restore Izzy's heart. I remember that night after we prayed, I dreamt that Izzy and I traveled to India and that Izzy had a successful operation. A few days later, a friend of my husband connected us with Dr. Proscovia Mugaba.

It is here that I want to introduce everyone to Dr. Mugaba, the first female accredited pediatric cardiologist in Uganda. All of us at LWB feel so fortunate to get to work with this remarkable physician to help children who have been born with cardiac defects. Dr. Mugaba graduated from medical school in Uganda in 2003, and then worked at a missionary hospital before getting her Masters degree in pediatrics. Over the next few years, she developed a keen interest in children's hearts, but at the time there was no fellowship in pediatric cardiology in her country.

Dr. Mugaba didn't give up on her dream, however, and soon landed a cardiology fellowship in South Africa at the University of Cape Town. Following that training, she was told that she could work in the field of pediatric cardiology, but that particular fellowship would not allow her to become accredited. She knew she could return to Uganda and immediately begin working, but she was determined to receive full accreditation in her chosen field. Dr. Mugaba defied the odds yet again by becoming the first non-North American surgeon to be accepted into the pediatric cardiology program at the University of Alberta in Canada. The program was extremely challenging, because some physicians did not believe that a doctor from a developing country could excel in a developed setting. Dr. Mugaba proved them all wrong, however, being awarded in her first year of training the Neal Gupta Award in Pediatric Cardiology in recognition of her compassionate bedside manner and her skilled ability to work with both patients and their parents.

In a country with 20 million children and only a handful of heart doctors, you can imagine just how busy this remarkable, fully accredited pediatric cardiologist is. Yet she treats each one of her patients as if they are her own child, carefully explaining each child's heart condition to their families and encouraging them to search for funding options through some of the medical NGOs.

Susan and her husband applied to multiple charities, asking for help for their little boy Izzy. They also applied directly to hospitals abroad to see if any of them would accept their son. None came through. Susan continues her story:

We were so desperate, knowing that time was running out and not even a ray of hope was anywhere to be seen. Dr. Mugaba called me one Sunday evening and told me about Love Without Boundaries. She gave me Director Ronald's number. She told me to call him and tell him about Izzy's condition, and also tell him that she had personally referred me to him. I immediately dialed his number, and he received me so well. He comforted me, and then gave me a form to fill out, which I did right away. I got an answer immediately, asking for Izzy's medical records. In just one evening, I was done sending all of his medical documents and the photos.

The next day, early in the morning, I found a WhatsApp message from Julia Bennett with LWB. It was then that the journey of comfort began. In just three weeks, a miracle happened. Izzy was accepted into the Love Without Boundaries' cardiac program. I was overjoyed! I immediately showed my husband what good news had come our way. I felt like I was dreaming. Something good had finally come for our Izzy! God was answering our prayers.

At that point in time, LWB was primarily using a hospital in Kolkata, India, for heart surgeries, and so we sent Izzy's records for evaluation. His heart defect was very complex, but the hospital felt a repair was likely.

Susan's story continues:

The acceptance into Love Without Boundaries was such a joy that even though I had never left the country of Uganda before, I was not scared. I was just so happy. LWB sent their travel groups with a registered nurse; so I wasn't worried about anything in the least. Madame Julia had comforted me so much. She had made me fully aware of how we would be well taken care of in India. However, my greatest fear of all was whether my son would come back alive from the surgery operation. Well, I told myself that I was going to be strong no matter what. I knew that God, who gave me Izzy, would still watch over him in the operating theater.

Our preparations began. Oh, I was excited! I kept telling my son that he was going to soon be well. The passports, the visas, the air tickets, and all the travel documents for me and Izzy were arranged by LWB. At that time, my husband had lost his job, as his boss said that he could not employ someone who had to take time off to care for a child with health issues. *In conversation with Madame Julia, I let her know about our sad situation, but she told us not to worry. Izzy's surgery would all be covered. Finally, the long-awaited day of January 7th arrived. We were flown to India, and it was such a joy!*

We had sent little Izzy with a group of six children from Uganda, who all had complex heart issues which could not be repaired back home. One after another, each of those precious children underwent surgery in Kolkata…all but little Izzy. Doctors had decided that since he was already almost a year old with a heart condition that should have been repaired as a small infant, they needed extra tests run to see if it would still be possible to successfully repair his heart. A few days later, the news from the heart doctor was devastating. He used the one word we never want to hear: inoperable. Susan continues her tale:

When I remember what it was like when the doctors in Kolkata said my son could not have surgery… the news hit me so hard! Oh God, why this? Could it be that I heard it wrong? How could it be? My son hadn't received his operation. He can't be discharged! I actually thought that when I was told to prepare to leave the hospital that they had passed on the information to the wrong person. Why would we be discharged when my Izzy wasn't healed yet?

I was filled with sorrow for my son. I cried at the thought of my son passing away. To see the other children receive their operations and then to know my son was rejected for surgery was just so painful. With so much sorrow, we packed up and headed back to the local apartment LWB had rented. My body grew so weak. I sent messages to my husband and told him we were coming back to Uganda. I sent messages to my pastor telling him everything that was happening. He gently told me to rest and know God was in full control.

One of the things that I have learned so clearly through my work with often extremely sick children is that a single strand of hope is still an immensely powerful thing. Little Izzy was still alive, and so we knew that, as long as he was breathing, hope was still alive. Our team contacted Dr. Mugaba back in Uganda and explained that the hospital in Kolkata had refused Izzy's case. She put us in touch with one of her favorite hospitals in India – Amrita Hospital, located in Kerala.

Amrita's pediatric cardiology program began in 1998 and is now considered one of the leading pediatric heart programs in India. Having performed over 13,000 heart surgeries, the surgeons at Amrita are confident in accepting children who have heart conditions with a high degree of complexity. We immediately sent Izzy's medical documentation to the Amrita team, and within 24 hours they had accepted him for surgery. I am sure you can imagine what this news meant to Izzy's mom Susan.

Madame Julia sent me a message that we were going to be flown immediately to Amrita. The doctors had said they would do their absolute best for my son. I was overjoyed. All the pain I was feeling in my heart and body suddenly disappeared, and I got strength again. I could once again smile, and immediately I began packing for our flight from Kolkata to Kochi.

However, even when we safely reached Amrita, I was still so worried. What if they also said that my son's heart was too damaged? What would become of my son? With time running out, I was still on my toes. Izzy was only three weeks away from his first birthday, and the cardiologist back in Uganda had told us that once he reached a year, nothing could be done to save him.

I am happy to report that Izzy underwent a very successful heart repair at Amrita. He actually recovered so quickly that he was able to meet back up with the rest of his travel group from Kolkata to fly back home to Uganda! This beautiful little boy's story could have ended so differently, as it seemed like almost every door to his healing had continued to close. But at the end of a very dark hallway, there remained a glimmer of hope that Izzy's wonderful mom held on to tightly. I continue to give thanks for sweet Izzy's life and that he is blessing the world with his presence each day. I also give thanks that from that small sliver of light, by sending the first LWB child to Amrita for surgery, an entire new program was formed.

You see, after we saw firsthand the skill and compassion shown at Amrita when Izzy's surgery was completed, we reached out to the cardiac surgeons there to discuss the possibility of also supporting Indian children at their facility. This was our chance to show "love without boundaries" to children with heart needs in India as well. We decided we wanted to be a charity that not only provides funding for the children…but on-the-ground emotional support for the families as well. We jumped right in, and by the very next month we had already provided healing to seven Indian children who had been born with congenital heart defects.

One of the first children we were able to support was a baby boy who had arrived urgently to Amrita after an eight-hour ambulance ride. The tiny baby, Sundeep, was suffering not only from pneumonia but also from a large hole between the lower chambers of his heart. His parents told our team that they had learned about Sundeep's heart condition when he was 4 months old, after he became extremely ill with a high fever. They were told by the doctors that they needed to save money because the waiting list for charitable help in their state was incredibly backlogged. Sundeep would not be able to survive that long. His parents tried their absolute best to come up with the funds for his surgery, but their son continued to decline. They were told their only chance was to make the journey to Amrita with the hope that a charity would agree to take the case. I am so thankful LWB was able to be the one who said, "Yes." Shortly after arriving at the hospital in critical condition, Sundeep had a very successful heart surgery. His mom was overcome with emotion, crying tears of joy. She took the hand of our LWB team member Stephy, saying simply, "Thank you for saving the life of my son." This is why we do this essential work and try our very best to continue building an authentic community...so that hope for both children and families can be restored.

After completing the first ten surgeries for Indian children at Amrita, we reached back out to Izzy's mom, Susan, to let her know that her little boy had laid the foundation for our newest cardiac initiative. She could not believe this piece of news.

As Izzy's parents, we feel so honored and privileged to know our own son has been used by God for the greater good. Who are we that God used Izzy in this way? It's such an honor, and we feel so glad that so many other lives are going to be positively impacted forever. More children will receive life-saving surgeries, and as a mother there is so much joy in knowing more children will be given a chance to live again just like my Izzy. I know God not only had my son in mind, but He wanted to reach out to other children as well. It is my greatest prayer that even more people will discover Love Without Boundaries so that more children globally will be healed.

I would also like to say thank you for looking so hard for a second opinion for my son. Thank you for not giving up on us. Oh...my...you fought this strong battle and won it for us. I can't wait for Izzy to grow up and I can tell him the complete story. The story of arrows and shields, the story of a battle so strong, and finally... the mighty cry of triumph and victory!

I would also like to send a big thank you to Izzy's donors, wherever they are. They changed my son's life. We are delighted by the love shown unto us, by people we have never even met. And to the LWB team, from Uganda to America to India and the rest of the world, thank you for reaching out to me and my family to keep asking how we are doing.

What a testimony of a baby, who received hope when it had all been washed away. He went from sitting and crawling to slowly rising up to stand. He can now laugh out loud, calling for his 'Dada' and 'Mom.' These were things that were simply impossible before. Long live LWB. Long live my darling Izzy.

Yes indeed...long live Izzy. And Sundeep, Emily, and Nora. This is one of my favorite parts of watching goodness be sown in the world. Seeds of true kindness build the most tenacious roots, and, with every new connection that is formed, even more lives can be impacted. It really is astonishing.

There's a very well-known song from the "Lion King" movie that has always meant so much to me. I can remember watching the movie with each of my children, with them sitting spellbound as "The Circle of Life" song would begin to play. Inevitably I would have tears come to my eyes when the first words were sung:

From the day we arrive on the planet

And blinking, step into the sun

There's more to be seen than can ever be seen

More to do than can ever be done.

Even typing those words now gives me goosebumps. What I love most about this song is that no matter how many times I listen, it always starts with light. With the image of every child on earth being welcomed by the sun. That to me is the true gift of hope. No matter how many times life tries to knock us down or despite how much pain is inevitably sent our way, there is still light to be found in this world.

Light that gives us the strength to somehow stand back up and face a new day.

We can never give up on the promise of hope. **For as long as there are children like the ones whose stories you have read in this book, children who are so deserving of people to believe in them, our life-changing work with LWB unquestionably must go on.**

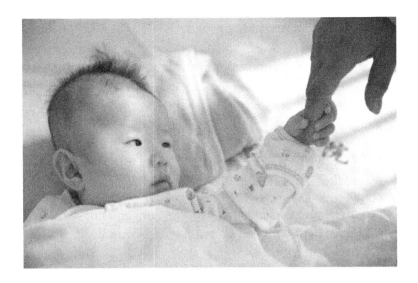

In Closing

Right as I was finishing up the last chapter in this book, my 86-year-old father handed me a small leather case holding the pocket-sized Dictaphone he had always carried with him on his job. I remember playing with it as a child when he wasn't looking, and I know there were times that he went to listen to his notes on an important meeting when suddenly the tape would jump to me saying "Testing, testing, testing" or to our dog barking at a squirrel. Sorry about that, Dad.

The tape he gave me, however, wasn't one of his work summaries. Instead, it was something he had saved for the last four decades. At the end of my senior year in high school, the principal had called me into his office to let me know I'd been invited to give the commencement speech at graduation. I think I made him a little bit nervous when I asked, "Am I allowed to say whatever I want?" I don't think I eased his worries a few weeks later, after being asked to submit the title of my talk to print in the program, when I smiled and told him the title was going to be one of the lyrics from a Neil Young song. He said, "You do know it's supposed to be a standard graduation speech, right? The definition of success, looking to the future, remembering the legacy of the last four years...." I nodded my head earnestly and assured him that I knew.

Now, almost 40 years later, I pressed "Play" on the tape recorder and got to hear myself as a teen. My family had never taken any video footage of us as children, so it was a bit surreal to be listening to my actual voice from all those years ago talking to an audience about what I believed was most important in life.

I think I must have let my principal down that afternoon as I didn't end up speaking about success, or leadership, or surprisingly even about high school. I sat in my desk chair and listened to a younger me instead talk about the vital importance of loving one another. I heard myself state, with an unexpected amount of confidence, that each of us is given such a limited time on this earth. Since none of us know when our last day will be, we can't wait until it's too late to let people know how much they mean to us. Eighteen-year-old me closed the speech with the following words:

The time to pick up the phone is now.

The time to write that letter is now.

The time to show love to one another...is now.

I closed my eyes after hearing my speech and took a few deep breaths. I never could have imagined all those years ago, standing in my high school cap and gown, with a completely unknown future in front of me, that I would someday get to be part of an organization dedicated to pouring out love for others. I had no way of knowing at the time that it wouldn't end up being university professors who would teach me the deepest lessons of life, but instead the thousands of children in our programs who continually take my breath away and make me strive to be a better person. Nor could I have imagined that my small circle of friends in Ohio would someday expand to extraordinary people around the globe...and to a community who understands that in a world too often riveted by division, war, and scandal that the real majesty of life comes through the redemptive power of love.

Listening to the tape had reminded me that when I was still just a child (as even at the end of high school that's really what I was), I had felt a powerful yearning deep in my soul. The same longing every child on this earth universally shares....to fully believe we are worthy of being loved.

What would life look like if we truly gave it our all to love other people? If we fed the poor, welcomed strangers, forgave each other, and loved others as if they were ourselves? As a teen, I was trying to better understand the virtue of authentic human connection, but now, many decades later, I'm fully aware of the vital importance of not closing ourselves off to others. We need one another, don't we? The time to show love truly is now, as each of us, no matter the scars our hearts might carry, has the ability to bring light to this world. We have the ability to support and create and lift up and heal. From our very first breath, we are born to be a blessing.

I hope through the stories in this book that I've managed in some small way to share the magnificence of humankind when love is put into action. I am humbled that I get a front row seat to see the important work being done by our international team members, the selfless commitment of our volunteers, and the incredible generosity of those who give to our projects. We shouldn't let the quiet acts of mercy happening all around us each day go unnoticed, as the more we come together with compassion and love, the more this journey of life has real meaning and joy.

I hope wherever you are on your own personal journey that you have found at least one authentic community of which to be a part. A community where you feel safe to contribute your God-given gifts to our world. A community that is filled with people who value your presence and who are there to offer encouragement when sorrow or sadness comes your way.

What I have learned through my work with vulnerable children around the world is that community, as we share it, doesn't always mean who lives next door. In fact, communities can protect and support each other even when separated by thousands of miles. A true community arises when people understand that the best stories of hope are those which are written together. It's people helping people…and nothing is more powerful, and beautiful, than that.

The Heart of Community

For more information about Love Without Boundaries and our work with vulnerable children, please visit our website at

www.lwbkids.org

"Every Child Counts"

Made in the USA
Columbia, SC
02 July 2021